Life with an Accent is based upon the memories of my

husband,

Frank J. Levy

and dedicated to:

Frank's Grandma, Alice Hamburger Levy, who was born in
Aschaffenburg, Germany, and who later reunited her two
sons and their families in America after WWII

and

Lou Ann Walker, my mentor and friend, without whom this
book would never have been written

and

The next generation, especially our eight grandchildren:
Margalit, Eliana, Yoni, Julia, Charlotte, Theo, Benjamin
and Annabelle.

i

Published by The Crescendo Group.

Available from www.amazon.com and other retailers.

An excerpt from *Life with an Accent* entitled "America 101" appeared in the spring 2009 edition of *The Southampton Review*.

LCCN: 2013908772

ISBN: 0989006107

ISBN-13: 9780989006101

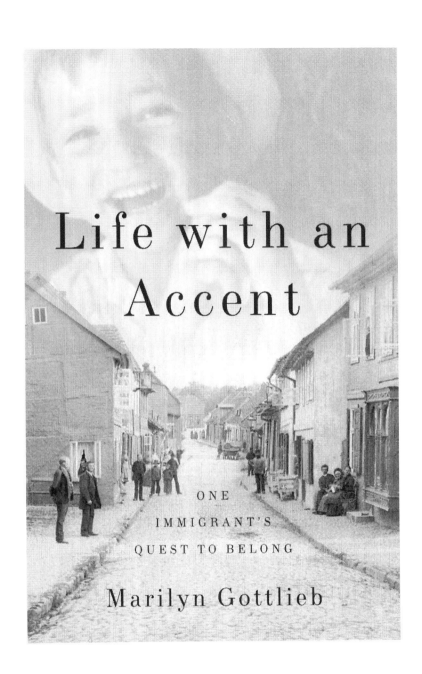

Life with an Accent

ONE
IMMIGRANT'S
QUEST TO BELONG

Marilyn Gottlieb

"Where are you from?" Gorbachev asked Frank.
"Where are you really from?"

Prologue: The Hamptons, 2008

We live in the Hamptons now, in a small safe haven on the South Shore of Long Island. But if you ask my husband where he's from, he'll tell you, with his distinctive intonation: "I'm half from Germany, half from the British Mandate of Palestine and half from America." I know it doesn't compute, but Frank's life has always been bigger than the whole.

Frank Berthold Jacob Levy was born a Jew in Berlin on November 3, 1933, the year Hitler was appointed Chancellor of Germany, almost three years before Frank moved to Palestine, 12 years before he immigrated to America, 48 years before cancer claimed his first wife and 50 years before his textile machinery business moved to China.

1933 was 57 years before we married and 75 years before Frank traveled to the European Parliament in Brussels where Mrs. Maneka Gandhi presented him with the 2008 World ENERGY GLOBE Award on behalf of the United States.

That's a lot to absorb, a lot of markers in the life of a man used to starting over, searching for a way to survive, yearning to belong.

And me, the All-American woman Frank married? I was born in New York on December 2, 1942, three years before the end of WWII. I followed fashion, not history. In high school I was the drum majorette leading the band, high stepping across the football field with a tall blue hat on my head, a whistle in my mouth and a baton in my hand. Growing up I was more familiar with Elvis Presley, Bob Dylan and the Beatles than The League of Nations or the establishment of the State of Israel.

Being Jewish meant dinner with the family for the New Year and Passover. What I knew about the Middle East I learned from watching Paul Newman in the film, *Exodus*. I went to a "good" college, married the day after I graduated, divorced two sons later and built a communications career in the world of advertising. I lived in Westchester most of my life. I never thought about belonging.

When I married Frank, I fell into a history book. I wanted to know his story, to share his memories even if they differed from information available elsewhere. I became aware of the effects world events have upon our lives. I accompanied him to Germany, though I don't like the sound of the German language, am pained by the country's history and am wary of its older citizens.

My husband is different. He likes everyone, including the elderly residents of Crivitz, Germany, where his grandfather lived until the Nazis took over. While there I watched Frank put his arm around the town historian's shoulder, as he is prone to do when making a point, engaging a stranger, pulling him into Frank's special world. I did not realize Frank would become friends with Dr. Fritz Rohde. I could not entertain the idea that Nazi actions had affected both their lives and I thought: *This man might have helped the Germans kill Frank's relatives. How can Frank be so nice?*

It was not the first time our opposing viewpoints collided. For years Frank has been assembling letters, photos, old plane tickets, coins, a Boy Scout badge, an old blanket, a swimming trophy and other keepsakes to make sense of his life. I thought of it as a sweet hobby to be shared with his grandchildren. Then my niece, Melissa, interviewed Frank for a college assignment. Her paper inspired me to learn more.

Frank reminisced. I listened. As he spoke, I took notes, asked questions, and verified facts online. Some checked out. Others seemed to have been created in his heart. I developed a renewed interest in his friends from around the world. When planning a trip, instead of flipping through travel books, I matched Frank's recollections to historical events in places we visited. Each excursion unleashed a flood of details long buried beneath the routine of everyday life. I collected so many they spilled into a book: This book.

Part I
Under The Radar of War
1933-1946

1: A Smooth Way Out

1934 August: Hitler becomes Führer (head of state) as well as Chancellor.

1935 The Nuremberg Laws strip German Jews of citizenship. Jews lose their right to use public transportation, restaurants, theaters and stores. Jewish children are banned from public schools.

1936 August: The Olympics are held in Berlin. Restrictions on Jews are lifted temporarily to give tourists the impression that all is well.

Frank's first memories are of Uncle Herbert giving him sunflower seeds to feed the pigeons in Venice. Hundreds, no, it might have been thousands of pigeons were flying everywhere. He could hear them coo above the sound of musicians playing their violins. I imagine his father, Fritz, and his mother, Hilda, waltzing in the piazza, perhaps a tear or two rolling down his mother's face, while Frank was fascinated by the birds.

"At the start the cooing was pleasant," he said. "Then it became a monstrous, unfamiliar noise jumbled with a bombardment of other new experiences."

The pigeons seemed to fill Piazza San Marco. They were bobbing their heads, pecking holes in the marble of the Basilica San Marco. They flocked toward him from every direction, nibbling at the seeds in his outstretched hands. He could hear them flapping their wings as they landed near his feet, on his shoulder, then on his head. He quickly figured out to drop the seeds, to stop feeding these scary birds even though his papa insisted, "Mucki, hold out your arms so the pigeons can reach the bird seed."

It was the end of August 1936 and photos show a little boy dressed in short white pants, a white shirt and light jacket with white shoes up to his ankles, a typical German outfit for an almost 3-year-old boy, the same outfit he had worn the day before on the train from Berlin to Venice. The next day he would continue his journey to Palestine, his new home.

This day in August was a day of rest. It was special because Frank was visiting with his only uncle who worked in Zurich and was vacationing in Cortina, not far from Venice. Frank's papa, in his jacket, starched white shirt and tie, wept as he hugged his younger brother goodbye. Frank was also crying, probably from fear of the birds, too young to understand a permanent separation.

"Don't cry," Uncle Herbert said. "Pigeons and doves are of the same family. They symbolize the peaceful land you are traveling to." Then he swept up his nephew and carried him to the shops that sold trinkets. "Pick something to help you remember today," he said as they walked through the ancient stone arches to look into store windows.

Frank told me he was thrilled to be safe in his uncle's arms, happy to get away from the birds with their iridescent feathers and bold intrusion. Most of all he was excited about selecting a new toy.

The uncle and nephew saw shop upon shop selling glass vases and figurines. They passed places that smelled of coffee and chocolate and stores that sold beautiful clothes. At first Frank was drawn to the red, yellow and blue glass items similar to the colorful Venetian glass vases that are now displayed under special lights in our built-in bookcase. Finally, Frank found something he really wanted. Maybe it reminded him of their neighbor's dachshund back in Berlin. Maybe it was just the right size for a small boy. Either way, it was to be his—a miniature black schnauzer that was an inch or two long. The toy dog had been carved from old wood and then painted black.

When Uncle Herbert and Frank returned, they joined Frank's parents for a walk along the Grand Canal, mingling with the tourists, enjoying the sounds of water lapping on the sides of gondolas and vaporettos that were competing for space in the dark water.

After Fritz and Hilda said farewell to Uncle Herbert, the family boarded another train to Trieste to meet a huge white passenger ship. At least it was huge in Frank's mind. Even though he wasn't quite 3, he remembers the festive atmosphere, the holiday feeling amongst most of the travelers. He was happy to be part of the fun.

"I climbed on anything that was climbable, so my mother put me in a harness with a leash for the two-day journey," he said. "Some passengers told her it was cruel, but I'm sure Mother just smiled and walked the deck with me in tow until we landed in Jaffa, at that time the only deep-water port in the area."

According to the story circulated within the family, an Arab rowed them to the coast, joking with Frank's papa that Hilda was too skinny to be a good wife. He said, "She is not even worth one camel."

Before descending the narrow wooden ladder in her heels, Mother passed her son to a man who had already found a seat in the vessel. As they approached shore the man lifted him in the air asking, "Does anyone own this child?"

There are no records of what happened next. The details of the voyage are lost forever. Frank was too young to remember much more and his parents hardly spoke about their peaceful escape.

In later years the Jewish National Fund and other organizations helped relocate families, often providing housing and land in small farming villages. But the Levys' arrival in Palestine preceded the big wave of immigrants. Hilda, Fritz and Frank were on their own.

We'll never know how Frank's parents, speaking only German, settled straight off the boat in this hot, dusty environment. I can picture his father walking down Ben Yehuda Street, the main avenue in Tel Aviv, carrying two suitcases, his elegant wife holding Frank and Frank clutching his little black dog. Eventually they rented a single room from a young Hungarian immigrant who cooked lunch for workers. Soon after they found an upstairs flat around the corner one block from the Mediterranean Sea.

Although they saw Herbert once in Palestine, the two brothers would not reunite for another ten years.

2: A Tough Decision

1933 January 30: Hitler is appointed Chancellor of
Germany. Within weeks the Enabling Act allows
Hitler to pass laws without parliamentary debate.

April 26: Hitler demands a boycott of Jewish
businesses and establishes the Gestapo—the Secret
State Police.

"What made your parents go to Venice?" I asked. "What gave them the foresight and courage to leave Germany so early?"

"My mother," Frank said, taking a step back to the beginning of his story. "My Mother pushed to get away from the Nazis and my father agreed."

Frank's mother, Hilda Pauline Jacobson Levy, was a formidable woman. She earned her Ph.D. in economics at the age of 80. Hilda wasn't a flirt, like my mother. She discussed politics, but she rarely discussed her life in 1933.

"Why?" I asked, craving details. "Didn't your mother explain the reason they left a few years after you were born, especially given that so many others stayed?"

"A little," Frank said, "but not as much as you'd expect. I learned more about my early life in Germany from history books. It's all there. Cold facts, except my parents lived much of what I read. If you dig into this time frame, you will ask why so many stayed rather than why my parents left."

So I turned to history books and checked online. It didn't take long to discover how difficult life was in 1933. That was the year of the burning of the Reichstag building––where Berlin's Parliament met. Hitler accused the Communist Party of setting the fire and used the incident as a means to curtail civil liberties. In 1933, the Gestapo—the Secret State Police—were formed and the Dachau concentration camp was opened to house political prisoners just ten miles northwest of Munich.

"I'm not sure my parents knew everything about their changing government until much later," Frank said. "They knew more about the personal liberties they were losing each day."

On May 10, when Hilda was pregnant, students in university towns throughout Germany torched and burned thousands of books to cleanse the country of un-German thoughts. They burned books by H. G. Wells, Karl Marx, Helen Keller, Bertolt Brecht and Heinrich Mann. Of course they included Jewish writings such as work by psychologist Sigmund Freud. They also burned academic papers written by Albert Einstein who had won the Nobel Prize in Physics. Nazi rallies proclaimed a new era in which Jews were blamed for all of Germany's problems.

"Joseph Goebbels addressed thousands of people in Berlin," Frank said, "inciting more book burning. Living in Berlin, of course, my parents knew about that."

Frank was born six months later. At the time, after childbirth women routinely stayed in the hospital for over a week. That explains why Hilda was still in a clinic when the brown shirts marched outside her window in preparation for the November 12th election.

"What was the vote for?" I asked Hilda one Thanksgiving when she was teaching me her mother's recipe for apple pie.

"The brown shirts were demanding support for Hitler's decision to withdraw from the Geneva Disarmament Conference and the League of Nations," she said. "I didn't want to back him. I had a private room and my nurse agreed to put a sign on my door: 'Patient is recovering from a serious operation and should not be disturbed.'"

I thought it was a risky move. If she had been caught, it was unclear what the Nazis would have done to the young Jewish woman. Perhaps she was not important enough to bother. Perhaps they would have vented their growing animosity. They already had ruled that Jewish doctors and dentists could not work with state-run insurance companies. Aryans were required to boycott their Jewish neighbors' shops, banks and other businesses. Hilda's refusal to vote for Hitler would have been a perfect opportunity for the Nazis to teach her and her family a lesson.

"They left me alone," she said. "I slipped under their radar, but I still had to deal with my parents. They were angry with me when I became pregnant."

"How can you bring a child into *this* world?" Marta and Martin Jacobson had asked.

By the time Hilda and Fritz took Frank home from the hospital, people were starting to get nervous about their neighbors.

"I was afraid to talk to my Aryan friends about anything," Hilda said. "We became wary of each other. Jews couldn't attend public events, not even the movies, so we went our separate ways. Friendships withered."

The Levys' two-family house was in a residential area called Hermsdorf on the outskirts of Berlin.

"I walked my baby along the sidewalks near our house," Hilda said. "The streets were lined with trees, stores and private homes like the suburbs here in America. Our porch was filled with pots of white flowers, adding to the peaceful façade that masked the poison springing up around us."

Mrs. Velzine owned the house. She lived below with her dachshund. She had no children of her own. Maybe that's why she liked to help care for Frank and fell in love with the little boy. Mrs. Velzine nicknamed him Muckelchen, meaning cute little one. The name stuck while they lived in Germany and I've been told she's the reason Frank is still called Mucki by some people.

In 1933 the Nazis began to attack Jewish stores. A year later Jewish children were banned from German public schools. Frank's mother was only allowed to buy meat during one two-hour period a week.

"I was forced to quit college," Hilda said, "even though I was the only female earning a business degree at my university, Handelshochschule."

The family printing, publishing and binding company was also in trouble. Frank's father, Fritz, was forbidden to work with German banks or the Berlin Stock Exchange.

"Without his two biggest clients, papa made no money," Frank said.

Amongst all the turmoil, Fritz and Hilda read Hitler's book, *Mein Kampf*, describing how Hitler would eliminate the Jews.

"If someone threatens to kill you," Hilda said, "you don't wait until they do."

Frank's parents decided to start over in a safer place. His father had visited Palestine on a hiking trip with his friends from the *Blau Weiss* Club, a Zionist sports club.

He felt familiar with that part of the world and Hilda...Hilda would go with her husband wherever he went.

The police station was adjacent to their backyard. In preparation for departure, Hilda had obtained the mandatory eagle and Nazi insignia stamped on their passports. But the police in Berlin-Hermsdorf were not happy about the supposed vacation. It took many attempts to get the proper documents, attempts Frank's mother hid from her Aryan friends.

"The man in charge knew us," Hilda said. "He grabbed Frank, saying, 'Palestine is no place to take a child. It's a country filled with tarantulas, scorpions and snakes. It is too hot for a little boy. Leave him behind and I'll watch him until you return.'"

Hilda kept calm. "No thank you. We will all stay here," she said as she took her son back into her arms.

They waited until there was a change of guard and then tried again.

"We felt there wasn't much choice," Hilda said. "It was almost a year after the Nuremberg Laws were implemented. Jews no longer were considered German citizens and we lost the rest of the rights that had been eroding all through Frank's short life. It was time to make a break."

Every Saturday the extended family gathered for a weekly afternoon *kaffeeklatsch*. An old photo shows them dressed in clothes that would be formal enough for a cocktail party. I could smell the coffee and imagine the apple strudel they enjoyed before Hilda revealed their plans to emigrate.

Hilda's uncle, Dr. Carl Joseph, yelled at her. "You are 27, an inexperienced, stupid young girl," he said. "Nobody needs to leave our country. Nobody needs to trade Beethoven concerts, theater, museums and Bauhaus architecture for life in the hot sand. Our family has lived in

Germany for hundreds of years. Your papa and I have been awarded the German Iron Cross for service in WWI. Certainly nothing bad will happen to us."

Was it an instinct for survival that motivated Frank's mother and father, not yet 30 years old, to resist the wisdom of their elders, to carry their toddler son along with a few valuables and leave? Just leave. Was it extreme intelligence that helped them find the strength to trade the familiar for a chance, only a chance, to breathe on?

It was early in the Nazi regime; before Jewish businesses were confiscated, so they sold a 40% interest in their printing company. Maybe that was the best they could do or perhaps they were pretending they would return. In later years Frank's parents told him that while Jews were still free to buy tickets they had applied to the German government for permission to travel through Italy to Palestine.

The Olympics were held in Berlin that summer. To keep up appearances for the outside world, signs reading "Jews Are Not Welcome" were taken down, and the Nazis eased anti-Jewish activities. Perhaps it was no coincidence that their passport gave the family permission to take their trip August 18 through August 24, 1936, shortly after the Olympics ended.

Hilda and Fritz smiled good-bye to their neighbors as if they were going on a short vacation to Italy. They walked out of their house, most likely holding Frank's hand.

"We closed the door to our home with everything in it," Hilda said. "We left our Citroën convertible in the driveway and never turned back."

3: A *Yekke* Starts Over, 1936-1939

1936 Arabs begin to revolt in Palestine. British military vehicles patrol the streets; British use guns to quell riots.

1938 Hitler is named Man of the Year by Time *magazine.*

Once in Palestine Fritz and Hilda assumed they would soon assimilate into their new homeland. It wasn't so simple. Some of the Jews, the Mizrahim, entered the British Mandate from neighboring countries: Iraq, Persia, Egypt and North African nations. Others, with Spanish roots, were the Sepharadim.

"I thought everyone was from Russia, Poland and the Ukraine," I said.

"They were the majority," Frank said. "They were called Ashkenazim and spoke Yiddish, a mixture of German, Hebrew and their local tongue as well as their native more formal language. They adapted. In the hot sun they wore shorts, sandals and hats."

In contrast, though the Germans were also Ashkenazim, they separated themselves. They clung to their more formal dress code.

12

"Despite the blazing Mediterranean heat, my mother wore heels," Frank said. "My papa wore his tie and jacket. I guess they were considered snobs, proud of their formal education and higher standard of living in the old country."

The German refugees reminisced about classical concerts, traditional and modern architecture and art they had left behind. Relationships with their Ashkenazi neighbors were strained.

"My parents wanted me to have an easier time," Frank said. "Maybe that's why they stopped calling me Mucki and began calling me Yaakov, the Hebrew version of Jacob that's one of the names on my birth certificate and a shortened version of Jacobson, my mother's maiden name. I'm sure they thought a Hebrew name would help me fit in."

In summer camp I had changed my name from Marilyn to Buzzy. I wouldn't choose that name today. It's not feminine and I'm a girly girl. I wanted a nickname and that was the first that popped out of my mouth. I don't know where it came from. The only Buzzy I had ever heard of and never met, was Buzzy Bavasi, the General Manager of the Brooklyn Dodgers whose son was in my fourth grade class in Westchester. I printed Buzzy on my sailor hat then forgot about it. Sometimes I didn't answer when my new friends called me. On visiting day my parents were stunned to learn there was no Marilyn Gottlieb at camp. Perhaps they meant Buzzy? My grown sons still laugh when an old buddy crosses my path and says, "Hi, Buzzy."

For me, it was all in fun. For Frank, a name change meant serious business. I'm amazed he didn't get confused when his parents still called him Mucki at home and his friends called him Yaakov in school. He claims he was comfortable with a new label to match his new country.

"My assimilation was slow and subtle," Frank said. "I remember when I started to call my parents *abba* and *ema*, the Hebrew words for father and mother. After that I never gave names much thought. I never had an identity crisis. Language, however, was a bigger issue."

The Germans didn't understand Hebrew, so they created their own German newspapers and spoke German amongst themselves. With the Nazis clamping down on Jews, it was understandable that other Jewish residents in Palestine despised the sound of German. Fritz and Hilda tried to remain quiet in public. They took night classes in Hebrew and Arabic, learning to read and write from right to left, but the teachers were barely ahead of their students.

"My parents encouraged me to learn Hebrew, too," Frank said. "My mother told me, 'When you buy an orange from a vendor, point to the fruit and ask how to say it in Hebrew.'"

The problem was a lot deeper than language. The German word for jacket is *jacke*, pronounced *yekke*. Since the men wore their suit jackets, *yekke* became the slang name to describe the German Jews in Palestine. It was not used in a positive way. Sometimes people yelled *yekke putz*. Germans were not just punctual. They were too punctual. They weren't simply polite. They were overly polite. Though their honesty was appreciated, they also were considered arrogant and humorless.

I had never heard the word *yekke* before I met Frank. I didn't *feel* what it meant until we ordered artichokes in a restaurant. My finished leaves were scattered on my plate; his were lined up in an order as precise as a blueprint. His knife and fork formed a perfect parallel. At home, I chopped onions and peppers in haphazard chunks, the faster the better. He took his time to chop even pieces. I tore my bread. He cut his, removing my ragged edges, subtle proof I had married a German.

The *yekkes* resisted assimilation, formed the German Immigrants Association and sought out other German Jews to befriend. Frank was part of this subgroup. Until he started school he didn't understand that he didn't fit in with the majority. As difficult as that was, his father faced a greater challenge—finding work.

While Fritz was attending college in Berlin, his father, Frank's grandfather, died. At 19 Frank's father had to quit school to take over the Berthold Levy Publishing and Bookbinding Company on Neue Friedrichstrasse 48. The company printed books, stationery, envelopes and index cards, as well as brochures and promotional material. It earned Fritz the respect of friends and neighbors and provided a good living—enough to support his mother and to pay for his kid brother, Herbert, to study textiles at a college in Zurich.

In the new country this experience was useless. He did not have the money to duplicate his business in the Middle East. Besides, nobody carried business cards. Fritz knew a German doctor who opened a grocery store and a German lawyer who started a chicken farm. For sure he'd find something. But what?

"My Uncle Herbert came up with a solution," Frank said. "Through Austrian friends he met investors in Vienna who wanted to build a bakery in Tel Aviv. Not just a simple storefront, but rather a nice-sized factory designed to sell fancy Viennese pastries as well as bread."

The investors purchased the baking equipment overseas and shipped it to Tel Aviv, then followed up with sugar, which was almost impossible to find in Palestine. All Fritz had to do was manage the Sova Bakery and sell the sweets wholesale to other shops, as well as to retail customers.

His delivery wagons were pulled by horses. Did he rent them? Own them? Feed the horses in a local stable? Nobody knows.

"All I remember," Frank said, "is visiting my father in the bakery and going for rides in the wagons while eating marzipan or chocolate pastry. Sneaking sweets was one of the first secrets my *abba* and I kept from *ema*."

The investors created a commercial about the Sova Bakery that is documented in the Steven Spielberg Archives at the Hebrew University in Jerusalem. The bakery building still stands, now a warehouse stocked with used furniture, and Frank still gravitates to marzipan whenever we find some in a bakery.

In 1938 Hitler closed Hilda's parents' rubber-recycling factory in Berlin. It was getting more dangerous for them to stay in Germany. *Opi* (grandpa) Martin Jacobson sold his machinery for scrap and he and *omi* (grandma) Marta Jacobson joined Hilda and Fritz in Palestine.

Omi's brother, Dr. Carl Joseph, the one who had yelled at Frank's mother for wanting to leave Germany, opted to remain in Berlin. He was in love with his sophisticated lifestyle and proud to be a medical doctor from the University of Heidelberg. He still didn't believe the events in Germany were permanent. He still didn't believe the situation would get worse.

Before the Jacobsons left they were able to ship a container of furniture, an enclosure 20 feet by 20 feet holding a washing machine, refrigerator, radio and other treasured items such as skis, coats, heavy shoes, towels, bed sheets and fur coats. I guess they hadn't considered the difference in weather.

They moved into Hilda's two-bedroom flat and shifted Frank to the living room. About the same time, in 1938, Frank's sister, Ada, was born. Their apartment was getting crowded.

"I couldn't understand why my parents were so excited to have a second child," Frank said. "I wanted a dog, not a sister."

In honor of her birth, *abba* gave Frank a box of chocolates. At 5 years old Frank was strong and determined to vent his disappointment. "I threw the box at the baby," he said. "*Abba* caught it before it hit Ada's head."

Instead of punishing his son, Fritz took Yaakov in his arms and assured him that one day he would have a dog—a guard dog, but today he had a new sister.

4: Kristallnacht in Germany

1938   November 9: Dr. Fritz Rohde, now a veterinarian and town historian in Crivitz, Germany, saw damage to a synagogue. His friend saw windows smashed in Berlin.

While Frank enjoyed a peaceful life in Tel Aviv, his future friend, Fritz Rohde, was a young Aryan boy living through sobering experiences under the Nazi regime in Crivitz, Germany. He was 15, too young for the military and too old to ignore what was going on.

If it hadn't been for the Nazis, as a child Frank probably would have accompanied his mother to Crivitz to see the family general store, as well as some distant cousins who lived north of Berlin. It is even possible that Frank would have become friends with Dr. Rohde, perhaps playing soccer with him. But the Nazis did exist, causing very different lives for the two German boys.

Aside from some travel to Jerusalem, including Yad Vashem, the World Center for Holocaust Research, Dr. Rohde rarely left his hometown.

"Maybe the trip to Yad Vashem inspired him to share his journal," Frank said. "Or perhaps there are other reasons we will never know."

Following is an excerpt from Dr. Rohde's unpublished private document, which Frank translated, titled: *Stories Through Which I Have Lived*.

Dr. Rohde wrote: One day my grandparents took me to Spandau with the SS Bahn train. From the train window I saw a large broken-down structure that had black burn marks on it with caved in sections. It was the synagogue on Fasanenstrasse in the heart of the city. Thousands of people were walking by this disaster every day. I stared at it, but most people turned away. As I gaped at this huge burned-out building, I yelled in shock, "What's happened there?" The faces of my grandparents turned into white stone. They looked straight and my grandfather pulled me away from the window saying, "This is not right what we are doing to the Jews. It will come back to us and will be a catastrophe. This fire will come back to us thousands of times."

Then my friend, who was 15, gave me a detailed report of what he saw in Berlin on Kristallnacht (The Night of Broken Glass) when he was with his uncle on a big boat full of apples. From a town called Aussig, they were moving along the Elbe River into Berlin to sell their fruit. It was night and he could hear people crying and yelling. He could hear breaking of windows and noise and thuds of people

19

being hit. In the morning my friend went into town to buy milk, coffee and cake. My friend said he was in complete shock seeing so many broken windows. The streets were full of glass. Beautiful stores were destroyed. The city was in total ruin. You could see well-dressed people hurrying past tall buildings carrying their purses across their chests. If they dropped their bags, you could see a big yellow star on their coats and see their faces. It was appalling.

So, we knew. Maybe not everything that was to come, but we knew. If we helped the Jews, we risked our own lives. But I always felt that we must put ourselves in their situation and try to understand how good citizens were required to be marked and put forward for destruction without any reason. Unfortunately this was not the end.

5: The Willys Goes To Abu Ghosh

*1939 The British MacDonald White Paper limits
immigration to Palestine.*

*The British blockade Palestine. Protestors
demonstrate in Tel Aviv.*

*Zionists organize illegal immigration to Palestine,
mostly by sea. Jewish refugees are kept at Atlit, a
barbed wire enclosed detainee camp.*

"It was still dark out as I opened my eyes and stepped onto
our cold tile floor," Frank said. "I usually got up when the
sun streamed into the living room where I slept."

It was Saturday, a day of rest for Orthodox Jews.
Shops in parts of Tel Aviv were closed and most public
vehicles were not allowed to operate in the Jewish sectors.
Only Arabic buses were running.

Frank's non-religious parents did not observe
Shabbat. On Saturdays they preferred to take the family on
outings to the beach or hikes to different villages within
two hours of Tel Aviv. They would walk along the Yarkon

River to the north, stopping at fields of sugar cane and flourmills powered by the river.

"This Saturday was even more special," Frank said. "My *abba* had bought a 4-cylinder Willys 77 and joined the Tel Aviv Automobile Club. I couldn't sleep knowing we were going to be part of a group that was driving to Abu Ghosh, an Arab village in the hills close to Jerusalem."

"In 1939, most people in Palestine didn't have cars," I said. "How did a Willys 77, made in Toledo, Ohio, get from America to Tel Aviv? How much did it cost?"

"I don't know," Frank said. "I was a kid, maybe 6 years old. I didn't care as long as I could ride in the car."

I understood Frank's love of automobiles. One of my favorite photos shows him as a little boy standing on the edge of his dad's Citroën when the family was on vacation in Marienbad, a spa town in the Karlovy Vary Region of what is now the Czech Republic. He was only 2 but he was already displaying an interest in vehicles and everything mechanical.

Today Frank drives a silver Lexus two-seater convertible, quite a difference from his dad's Willys. The Lexus replaced Frank's small silver BMW Z4 that had replaced his even smaller green BMW 323i that had replaced his 1984 red Targa.

"My favorite was my 1956 antique silver Porsche Cabriolet," Frank said. "It sputtered and smoked, but I loved it."

I was afraid to go along for a ride in the Cabriolet, so Frank traded his Porsche passion and the smiles it brought for safety and a chance to tool around together. On a top-down day he volunteers to drive to the West Hampton Cleaners on Mitchell Road, the Beach Bakery and Rite Aid Pharmacy on Main Street with the wind blowing whatever hair he has left on his head.

Did Frank inherit his love of cars from his dad? As a hobby his nephew, Josh, restores old cars and bikes. Maybe it's in the genes. Frank can recall details of every car he and his father owned.

"Our Willys was light blue," Frank said. "We lined up with more than ten cars and families to motor together along the unpaved corridor. We estimated it would take three to four hours through rugged terrain in the Judean mountains."

"This was just before WWII broke out," I said. "There were Arab revolts, violent underground Jewish groups and a ship full of illegal immigrants from Romania trying to land in Tel Aviv. Weren't you—or at least your parents—afraid to move about the land?"

"No, I knew my parents would take care of me," Frank said. "At the time of our road trip I didn't pay attention to world events and how they affected my life. I saw that streetlights and car lights were turned off at night, but my parents downplayed the reasons. They said it was safer and that was good enough for me."

"Didn't you ask how that made you safer?"

"No," Frank said. "We never talked about potential enemy bombers locating our roads by following lights. Air bombings and air raids came later. I didn't grasp how serious everything was. I just knew we had to leave early in order to get back before dark."

"How did people avoid hitting one another while driving down shadowy streets?"

"All the cars had white stripes painted on their fenders," Frank said. "Drivers could see the stripes as they got closer. I was never on the road after dark and since we left so early, I was sure we would be home during daylight. All I thought about was the trip. It was my first time as part of an entourage."

Some vehicles made it up, winding 3,000 feet above sea level. The Levy car didn't. Their beloved Willys boiled over in the heat. Water dripped out and they were forced to roll down the hill until they found help.

"As we approached Tel Aviv, we saw lots of jeeps and tanks," Frank said. "At first I wasn't scared because we often saw soldiers and military vehicles in our neighborhood. But this was different. It was quiet except for the sound of soldiers marching back and forth holding rifles, making sure nobody came in or out of the area. They looked so tall and fierce. No other people were in the streets. The city was closed."

A soldier stopped them.

"I huddled in the back seat," Frank said. "As young as I was I knew it was not a good time to ask questions."

One jeep moved in front of the Willys, another followed, forming a three-car caravan.

"We were escorted all the way to our apartment," Frank said. "We had to stay inside for three days while the soldiers searched door-to-door for illegal people and members of the *Haganah*, an underground group of Jewish militants who worked secretly to help displaced persons find safety."

"And you still weren't scared," I said.

"A little, but you have to understand," Frank said, "seeing British soldiers carrying guns was normal. My *ema* and I always ignored them when we walked to the beach where we refreshed ourselves with mashed bananas covered in sour cream. If we timed it right, I got to see the zookeeper walk his big black bear on a chain at the edge of the sea."

On September 1, 1939, Germany attacked Poland and started WWII.

"It was far away," Frank said. "The world was in turmoil but information didn't travel quickly."

There was no Internet, no TV and very few phones or radios. News came from the London BBC radio station, but was often interrupted by static. Most people didn't speak English, so it took even longer for reports to be translated and circulated.

"It must have been chaotic."

"I guess," Frank said.

Around this time the British came out with the MacDonald White Paper limiting the number of immigrants allowed into Palestine. The newspapers reported stories of refugees stranded on ships without enough food or water, unable to dock and unable to go back to the countries from which they had come. The ships floated on the sea while the passengers used up their limited provisions. There were rumors that some immigrants managed to sneak ashore and hide.

Jews held mass demonstrations against the policy of limiting refugees. Frank's mother thought uncontrolled crowds in Tel Aviv were dangerous. She wouldn't let him out to play.

"My mother later told me she was convinced that the potential for violence was greater in Tel Aviv than in a smaller village. Besides, with my new sister and grandparents living with us, we were out of room. It was time to move."

Once again, they got out under the radar of war, just months before the Italians bombed Tel Aviv in the middle of the day. Many families opted to go north to Kfar Sirkin, a Jewish stronghold during the Arab Revolt and headquarters for the *Haganah*. Others went to Ra'anana, a center for orchards or to Kfar Shmaryhu, along the coast.

Fritz and Hilda chose to go the other way, south of Tel Aviv and just south of a medieval Arab port city called Jaffa, strategically placed about 130 feet above the sea. It is an area rich in history with tales of Turkish, Egyptian, Greek, Hebrew, Christian, Roman and Muslim events that took place in Jaffa, from Jonah and the whale to St. Peter raising Tabitha and the Crusaders marching through the area as well.

In the mid-1930s Arabs were fighting against British rule and mass Jewish immigration. The British retaliated. They gutted beautiful light stone buildings on some of the most important streets in Jaffa. On one of our later visits to Israel we took my son, Michael, on a stroll along those same streets.

"It's all been rebuilt," Frank said as we wandered in front of houses and artists' shops along steep winding alleyways and narrow cobblestone paths lined with pots of brilliantly-colored flowers.

We paused in sight of the ancient clock tower that still stands in the central square.

"I think the Ilana Goor Museum is near here," Frank said. "On Mazel Dagim Street."

Ms. Goor is the award-winning artist and sculptress who designed the limited edition iron base for the shelf nestled behind our couch back home. While Michael and I ambled through her museum, we could feel the past inside the 18th century building with its high ceilings and stone arches that separate numerous rooms. I turned to share a thought with Frank, but he was gone. He had found Ms. Goor near her shop and had stopped to speak with her in Hebrew.

"I marveled at her work and the unique items that were for sale," Frank said.

Of course he also volunteered details of his early life not far from Jaffa and smiled his warm way into an invitation for all of us to visit her private living space that was adjacent to the museum.

"I think I see my old town," Frank said, gazing from her balcony overlooking the aquamarine sea. His enthusiasm fueled Ms. Goor to give us a complete tour of her home.

"Look at her Primus burners," Frank said pointing to a counter in her kitchen. "My mother once cooked on these." We had to pump it to make it work. It let out so much black smoke we repainted the kitchen every year."

Nothing like our Viking back home, I thought.

As Michael snapped photos of the Primus with his Canon 5D and 24-70 mm lens I knew he would buy a Primus in the flea market for Frank to bring home.

"The Primus was just one tiny difference between then and now," Frank said. "You can't imagine how undeveloped our new village was when my parents and grandparents hired movers, stuffed the Willys with their smaller belongings and drove beyond Jaffa to a town called Bat Yam—*Daughter of the Sea*.

The village had been founded in 1926 by a small group of Orthodox Jewish families—a heritage that would prove difficult for Frank coming from a non-religious family.

6: Bat Yam, Daughter Of The Sea

*1940 Germany's ally, Italy, attacks British in Palestine;
bomb Tel Aviv and Haifa.*

1941 Germans establish extermination camps in Poland.

"In Bat Yam my parents rented a two-bedroom concrete
house with stone walls and tiled floors," Frank said as we
walked along Balfour Street in search of his old home.
"This is nothing like where I grew up amidst the noise of
cars, buses and taxis."

The city overflowed with people meandering on
sidewalks adjacent to tall buildings.

"When we moved here in 1939, there were about
1,500 people, two synagogues, my eight-room schoolhouse
and a brewery all within walking distance from the
Mediterranean. Our home was the last house off a sandy
path at the end of the main paved road. The wind
sometimes changed the shape of the dunes and the white
sand was everywhere—in the yard, on our two open
porches, on the floors inside the house, inside my shoes,
even in my ears and hair."

The kitchen was the pride of the family. The Levys had an electric refrigerator and a washing machine. "In my six-year-old mind I thought it was six feet long, four feet wide and five feet tall, taller than I was," Frank said. "Inside was a round horizontal perforated cylinder. The cylinder turned in water—20 times to the right, then 20 times to the left. I counted. Under this machine were eight oil burners to boil the water. I counted those, too."

Signs of a future engineer, I thought.

Frank's mother had to light the burners each time they were used. Every Friday he helped drag the huge machine into the backyard and filled it with water from a short hose connected to a water pipe.

"We took turns holding the hose."

When everything was washed, Frank's grandmother hung the clothes and linens out to dry in the hot Middle Eastern sun. Then, in the best German tradition, she ironed every piece of laundry—underwear, sheets, shirts, tablecloths, even socks. All had to be pressed. And, despite their stark location, they still used crisp tablecloths and his *opi* still wore socks.

"Where did you sleep?" I asked.

"In the living room," Frank said. "Just like in Tel Aviv. The house was bigger than our apartment, but I still had to sleep in the living room."

"Didn't you feel cheated?" I asked.

"You have to understand—it's all I knew," he said. "I was content."

Frank's parents and sister shared one bedroom and his grandparents stuffed their German antique furniture into the other bedroom. At night their sofa opened into a double bed. During the day it was closed and the linens were placed inside two matching wooden carved boxes on each side of the couch, allowing their bedroom to serve as a second living room.

"Their carved dresser with ornate rosettes was bulky," Frank said, "but my mother thought it gave the house a stable feeling. All the furniture had wooden legs. When it was very hot I got to splash a bucket of water on the tiled floor. That's all we needed to cool the room.

Their only carpet, a fancy oriental rug, was spread out only in winter months when they didn't need to cool down. Having such a rug in this hot environment was one of many reminders that Frank's family didn't quite fit in.

"Another difference was our rabbits," Frank said. "Owning a house meant we had a backyard and were able to keep wooden cages sheltering 50 rabbits. We started with one pregnant rabbit, a 40-inch Belgian named Funny."

"Funny sounds like an English name," I said.

"Could be. I don't know where the first rabbit came from. Since it was nearly impossible to buy meat, we sold some and ate some. Rabbits are not kosher so at my religious school I got a terrible nickname: *Schafan*, ("Rabbit"). I hated it because it made me feel different."

"But you told me you had to eat what you grew or what you raised."

"Yes, that's why I felt it was not right for my friends to tease me for eating our rabbits," Frank said. "I loved the taste as much as I liked chicken, but we needed to save the ten chickens so we could have a continuous stream of fresh eggs."

"Maybe they were jealous," I said, though eating cute little bunnies was not something I wanted to defend. I had to stop myself from hissing "Yuck!" when Frank ordered *coniglio* on business trips in Italy.

"Since we had a hose we could water plants," Frank said. "That meant we could grow vegetables in the sand. Between the garden, the rabbits and the chickens we were able to live off the land."

Still, money was scarce. Frank's *opi* bought a donkey and cart to transport oranges and crates for farmers in Ra'anana, about 90 minutes away by bus. *Opi* parked his donkey and cart with his nephew, Heine, who had come to Palestine after his father, Alfred, was killed in the German army defending Germany in WWI. Heine and his wife had young children, a son named Avi and a daughter, Tova.

"I knew them even though they lived in Ra'anana near the orange orchards," Frank said. "*Opi* worked every day to bring home extra cash. It wasn't enough because the bakery where my dad worked in Tel Aviv was not doing well.

"It was hot where we lived. Maybe the heat discouraged people from eating heavy sweets. Maybe it was the price. Sugar was expensive, so the desserts were expensive. People struggling to survive economically didn't splurge on cakes."

The Viennese technical manager liked his job and did not want the bakery to close, so he created two sets of books. One was accurate and showed losses. The other proved a non-existent profit. When the owners came to Tel Aviv to see what was going on, the technical manager wanted to show them the fake books.

"My *abba* would have nothing to do with such dishonesty," Frank said, "so he left, even though it meant our family would have no income."

Soon after, the British confiscated the Sova building to house munitions. The investors lost their money.

Frank's mother found a job as a bookkeeper at Lewen-Epstein, a printing plant in Bat Yam. The cooking and daily chores fell to *omi* while *opi* took care of the animals and the shopping when he wasn't in Ra'anana.

"My *abba* had a difficult time finding a job," Frank said. "You have to understand. It was 1939 and the intertwining of Arab and Jewish economies was disintegrating and separating. More important, my *abba* needed a certificate of employment from Germany."

"Why didn't your mother need such a certificate?" I asked.

"I'm not sure," Frank said. "Maybe because she hadn't been working in Berlin when I was very young. Remember, when we left Germany, we pretended we were going on vacation. The Germans would have been suspicious if *abba* had tried to obtain references before a holiday trip."

Frank's father had written to the Passport Control Center in Berlin. Eventually he received a letter of reference. Was it because he had left Germany before the start of WWII or had his request simply landed in a sympathetic hand?

Through a German friend Frank's father found a job in a Tel Aviv bank. He kept that position for over a year, but then things got tougher. In the summer of 1940 the Italians started to bomb the British Mandate of Palestine primarily in Tel Aviv and Haifa, as well as coastal towns, including nearby Jaffa.

"On September 9, 1940 my parents were scheduled to meet in a restaurant," Frank said. "At the last minute *abba* cancelled due to another appointment, a lucky situation because the restaurant was bombed while they were supposed to be enjoying their meal.

Unbeknownst to Frank, Uncle Herbert and Frank's dad had begun to plan how to reunite in America. It would take another six years for their dream to be realized.

"In spite of what I later read about this era, for me it was the best of times," Frank said. "I liked my new school, a one-story stone building with a sandy soccer field on the side where, in bare feet, I played with my friends. I had no interest in leaving."

By now we were standing in front of a two-story edifice near a playground.

"I used to attend this school," Frank said in Hebrew to the female guard behind a locked iron gate. "Can we take a look?"

"I need to check with the principal," she told Frank, then she said something to me in Hebrew.

"I don't speak Hebrew," I said in English.

She nodded then disappeared. Less than five minutes later she returned.

"You can come in." She shifted her gaze toward Michael who was carrying his professional camera around his neck. "No photos," she said in English.

The principal met us halfway down a spotless linoleum hallway. The pale creamy walls were embellished with children's artwork: paintings of trees and colorful flowers planted in Israel.

Once again Frank conversed in Hebrew before we were escorted upstairs to a second-grade classroom. All the children stood and greeted us. A teacher asked them to sing a welcome song in respect to an older person. A young blond boy raised his hand and asked a question.

Frank smiled and interpreted for me: "The boy wants to know if I am 100 years old."

"Hardly," he told the boy. "But I can tell you a story from many years ago when I was little. We had fewer than 200 students in the whole school—grades one through eight. We all lined up facing the center of an open-ended sandy yard so our principal could check us for clean hands, ears and nails, polished shoes, combed hair and a handkerchief."

The children stared at Frank, then moved their eyes toward Michael and me.

"Our pants had buttons," Frank said. "I had never seen a zipper on men's trousers so while the principal examined us, I focused on the modern zipper on his dark blue suit. And I hoped I was perfect because if I didn't pass inspection, I would be sent home and forced to return with one of my parents."

Frank paused, engaging the young students. "If my parents had to come to school because of my behavior, they would be reprimanded in front of everyone."

After our visit Frank continued to reminisce.

"It was hard for me. The Orthodox boys had been reciting morning prayers all their lives. School was easier for them. I struggled to learn the prayers in Hebrew. My parents couldn't help, so I kept my head down. My prayer was that nobody would call on me. It didn't always work."

Frank hated school that first year. German letters are different from Hebrew letters. His parents read German from left to right. Frank was learning to read and write Hebrew from right to left, which felt backward.

"Nobody at home could help me."

Frank found understanding with his best friend, Yecheskiel (Chezzi) Cohen, who also had German parents.

"Neither of our families observed Orthodox rituals. It was natural for us to gravitate toward each other. We formed a bond as close as family."

7: Keeping Germans Quiet

1936 Elections in Germany confirm support for Hitler.

As Frank told me more about his childhood in Palestine, I thought about another segment of the parallel memoir Dr. Rohde had shared with us:

> Crivitz is in the Northeast German district of Mecklenberg. In 1932 the fanatic Nazi Mayor, Dr. Otto Boucke, was in charge of this territory that had some heavy Nazi involvement. In the 1930s Hitler drove through our area a number of times. Often he came from a nearby city called Schwerin. From the airport he paraded by with the SA guards who wore steel helmets. They were accompanied by various national German organizations, including the military. Hitler continued on to Severin, the small Mecklenberg village where Goebbels married his wife, Magda, in 1931. During the ceremony, it is said the pastor concealed the church cross with a Nazi Swastika.

Many people believe that Goebbels was responsible for Kristallnacht. In 1945 Goebbels poisoned his six children then shot his wife and himself.

One time, when Hitler drove through Crivitz with an entourage of automobiles, I stood with my mother and my childhood friend Rudy Baumgarten watching the parade. At the corner of Weinberg and Breidscheidstrasse, when Hitler's car came by, someone yelled out while raising his fist, "Down with Hitler." Immediately all the cars stopped.

To the shock of everyone watching at the edge of the street, SS guards jumped out of a car and pushed themselves into the crowd, yelling loudly. They barged into the house where the protester had run. He escaped out the back and disappeared into the crowd, but I had never seen such an explosive reaction. The SS could not find the protester and finally went back to their caravan and left. For sure this was not the only time people tried to protest Hitler.

In 1942 Russian soldiers told us they had seen people shot and pushed into graves. Women tried to save their children by pulling up their skirts and giving away their jewelry. The soldiers laughed when they took the offerings, then shot the women and children anyway.

In 1944 I was confirmed. There was beautiful organ music in our church and it was beautiful weather outside. We could hear the rumble of many planes dropping bombs nearby. Above was death. Below was a confirmation. It was strange. The worst was that no matter what we saw or heard, we had to remain mute or we would be eliminated, too.

8: A Letter from Dr. Carl Joseph

1942 January 20: Senior Nazis meet in Wannsee, a suburb
of Berlin, to determine the "Final Solution" for
Jews—ridding Europe of all Jews first by
deportation then by extermination.

Mass murder of Jews by gassing begins at
Auschwitz.

In 1942, back in Berlin, Hilda's uncle, Dr. Carl Joseph, composed a goodbye letter to his only daughter, Beatrice, in Johannesburg before he was deported to the Theresienstadt Concentration Camp in Czechoslovakia. Somehow he was able to mail the letter to his daughter who had already fled to South Africa. After his daughter read the letter she sent it to her aunt Marta, Frank's grandmother, in Bat Yam who later gave it to Frank.

October 9, 1942, just before deportation.
My most beloved Children:
On the 15th of this month the three weeks will be over that have been promised to me for the repair of my teeth. Then we

38

will have to abandon our home, leave behind all of our possessions and all that is dear to us and all that we acquired at great expense for an uncertain, definitely unpleasant destiny.

On the 21st of September we were suddenly informed that we must prepare all of our medical instruments for pick up. In the evening we received a document requiring us to list all of our estate, funds and furniture as well as lists of linens and clothes. In addition, we received orders to present ourselves on Sunday for transport to Theresienstadt near Prague. We are to be listed under the Transport Number 10894 and told this number is very important for follow up at the Cultural Agency or the Federal Organization.

The profound sadness was unimaginable. Even though we expected our fate, facing reality was shattering. Not only does it mean that now we have to give up all of our comfort and every cultural and hygienic practice but also our personal freedom. Consider the prospect of absolute poverty, the life of a beggar among beggars, a life under police surveillance and barbed wire, a life of insufficient nourishment and hard labor; consider the arbitrariness of the price demanded by those who call us their enemy.

We can only take with us the most needed items and soon thereafter we will be clothed in rags. Although Theresienstadt is considered to be the Eldorado, where only those over 70-years-old and the sick are accepted, in contrast to the prospects in Poland, where aside from the more severe weather, the dirt and the vermin, the labor is much harder and one would be deprived of community and probably moved frequently.

We hope that the three-week delay will not deprive us of going to Theresienstadt as doctors are sent wherever they are needed. We expect to see many friends and patients in Theresienstadt, among them Tante Ida who has been there for a few months. Also Walter L. who left about a month ago. Even in Theresienstadt, as far as we have learned, there is no free access among the individual building blocks.

At the end of a lifetime filled with work, this is what our future looks like. Only one thought enables us to continue and that is that we will get our life back, that we will survive all these terrible things and be reunited with you. No wonder that faced with such unimaginable and undeserved horrific destiny, many have lost their nerve and have voluntarily ended their existence.

Ultimately, only we are to blame that we are still here and did not pursue our emigration in a timely and energetic fashion.

We have named you as our beneficiaries in our will, but sadly we will not have anything in our estate. We have to leave all our possessions here. . . .I own nothing more than a few rags that I am wearing and which I carry in a small suitcase. They will hardly last till the end of this terrible war. I hope that it will be superfluous to mail this letter and we ourselves will appear in its stead. Once more, be well and remember our love of old,

Your loyal (trusted) parents

9: Who Will Help?

1942 First American troops land in North Africa.

1943 July 10: Allies land in Sicily. Mussolini resigns.

The trouble started when an undertow pulled Chezzi's dad, Mr. Cohen, further out to sea. It was a glorious Mediterranean day. The sun sparkled on the ocean filled with people swimming and bobbing in the 80-degree water.

"The waves were stronger than usual, but that didn't bother me," Frank said. "I was already 10 years old and a very good swimmer."

Bat Yam is situated along 3.5 km of sandy beaches. In 1943 Frank believed Arab and Jewish communities lived in peace near each other even though they were still monitored by British soldiers. Arab men in long robes with *keffiyehs,* those headscarves they wear to protect themselves from sun and blowing dust, mingled freely among the Jews. Clusters of Arab women wore headpieces with long black embroidered dresses. They carried huge wicker baskets to bring home fruits and vegetables bought in the markets.

"Jaffa was so close we could see the tops of some minarets and hear the calling of the faithful Muslims to pray five times a day," Frank said. "Sometimes we listened to bells worn by camels parading one behind the other on the sandy shore."

A donkey and an Arab led the procession North from Gaza loaded up with grapes to sell in the open markets. Small rugs and saddles in hues of dark reds and browns added to the colors of the caravan.

To make sure Frank stayed safe living so close to the water, his *abba* taught him how to swim at an early age. He set up a harness and hung Frank from the top of the living room door on a chin-up bar so he could move his arms and legs in the proper way.

"I had no idea this was unusual, Frank said. "It was how I learned to coordinate my breaststroke. I moved my arms forward, snapping my legs shut at the same time. I could glide through the water with the least resistance, confident I was faster than all my friends."

To build up his strength his *abba* made Frank swim half a mile from a huge boulder, called Adam's Rock, to a smaller stone, called Eve's Rock. And then he had to swim back. When he conquered that great distance, he was allowed to go to the sea with his friends.

On this day Frank was with his *abba* and Chezzi and Chezzi's father. *Abba* enjoyed gentle drifting. Chezzi didn't like the waves, so he swam back, content to sunbathe and watch from shore. Suddenly Mr. Cohen lost control and was dragged out by the tide. *Abba* and Frank were fine, but Chezzi's father shouted for help.

"My *abba* tried to put his arm around his friend's chin to pull him in," Frank said, "but his friend was frightened and from where I was, it looked like they were fighting in the water."

"Yaakov! Swim to shore and get help!" yelled his *abba*. "Swim as fast as you can. Use everything I taught you to bring help!"

Although Frank was petrified, he knew he could make it in very quickly. He swam and swam. He kicked his legs as fast as he could. He moved his arms as rapidly as possible. He wasn't sure it would be quick enough, so he tried harder and swam faster. He made use of the waves to slide forward, but the undertow was strong and pulled him back. He kept going.

The first people Frank saw on shore were two British guards standing in the water with their pants rolled up. Their armored cars were on top of the dunes and their rifles rested with their friends on the beach. They, too, were enjoying this glorious Mediterranean day. The British, who seemed to be everywhere, were not well liked by the Jews or the Arabs. Most likely the young soldiers did not want to be in Palestine, which might have added to so much tension among the different groups.

"Sometimes—I imagine it was for fun—the militia would shoot bullets into the sea over the heads of the swimmers."

After swimming ashore Frank was so out of breath he could hardly talk, but he knew he had to spit out his message. Of course he did not speak much English so he pointed to his *abba* and shouted, "Help!" in Hebrew and German.

The British soldiers looked at him then turned their blue eyes out to sea and watched the two men shout and flail their arms. The guards didn't move. Someone was drowning, but the soldiers were not interested. They made no effort to help. They made no attempt to get their friends to rescue Mr. Cohen. One flicked his wrist toward Frank as if Frank were a fly he was shooing away. Other soldiers surveying the scene from the top of a nearby dune also made no effort to help.

"I was furious. More than that, I was scared," Frank said. "I was scared for Chezzi's father and angry with the soldiers. I was angry with all the British and I wanted to throw sand at the guards—kick their ankles that were in my reach—but I knew I had a more important mission. I knew I had to find help and find it fast."

Nearby he saw senior members of the *Hapoel* Sailing Club, the youth group to which he belonged. He told them the trouble and without any hesitation the men raced into the waves, head first. Within minutes they brought back Frank's *abba* and Mr. Cohen.

"By then our neighbor, Matalon, a dark-skinned Jew perhaps from Yemen who also was a good soccer player, ran over to see if they were okay. Even a British soldier, the one holding an extra rifle, came to check on them. Suddenly, people from all different groups were gathered around offering drinks of water and help."

Chezzi was sent home to boil potatoes for dinner. Frank and his *abba* walked down the sandy unpaved road to their concrete house to take a hot shower before eating their main meal of vegetables from their garden with an orange for dessert.

"My *abba* used to tell me," Frank said, "if the end is well, all is well. With so many diverse groups living side by side, skirmishes existed in our land all the time. I was learning to live with them."

10: Selling Kites

*1943   February: Russians defeat Germans at the Battle of
        Stalingrad, beginning the eventual victory by Allies.*

By 1943 Frank was more assimilated in his new land than
his parents or grandparents.

"I didn't remember Germany," Frank said. "Bat
Yam was my home and I felt older than my ten years
because I could navigate our neighborhood with ease. But
if I wanted to buy something, I became a little boy again
and had to ask my parents for money. I yearned to earn my
own spare change. Other times I was content when my
grandfather slipped me some cash."

Once a week Frank's *opi* went to the *souk*, the
open-air market in Jaffa where Arab vendors hawked
oranges, pomegranates, vegetables and clothes from their
stalls. Sometimes Frank was allowed to tag along.

"My favorite part of these trips was going to an
Arabic restaurant, just the two of us, eating *shaslik* and
shish kabob. I was not permitted to tell anyone in our
family. Back home *opi* and I would look at each other in
silence, guarding our secret as we ate a second dinner."

If our excursion were on a Saturday, my *abba* and I would slip outside the *eruv*, the thin wire that surrounded the town overhead. As long as the Orthodox Jews remained within the encircled enclave on their Sabbath, they were allowed to use baby strollers and walking canes to move about the property. The *eruv* enabled them to adhere to their traditions with a little more flexibility.

"I was happy my family didn't follow this tradition," Frank said. "Every week we crossed the wire and ventured outside."

Each outing was an adventure. Frank never knew what he would find. If only he had some spare change in his pocket in case he passed a store with small toys or trinkets.

"One time our family walked to Jaffa to board an Arab bus that carried people, chickens, small goats and sheep," Frank said.

"Do you really mean that goats and sheep were inside the bus?" I asked. "It just can't be. I don't believe it."

"Yes," Frank insisted. "And chickens."

"Okay, I believe the chickens, but not the goats or sheep," I said, deciding to let it go. It's a second marriage and I've learned to choose my battles.

"You can imagine the smells that filled the hot air," Frank said. "And the yelling. That's what I remember."

The goods the Arabs carried were wrapped in sheets with the four corners knotted together to create a cloth container. The tops of the buses were fitted with huge luggage racks filled with all sorts of belongings: old suitcases, wooden crates, bags made out of the sheets perched precariously on top as the buses swayed to their next destination.

The bus dropped Frank and his family off in Lod where they started to hike to Kfar Sirkin, a village to the North where the Eldens lived.

"I think they are cousins," Frank said. "On my father's side."

"It doesn't matter," I said. "As my oldest son, Michael, always says, 'If you are fortunate enough to be a friend of Frank Levy you are, indeed, a relative and member of his family. What a great place to be.'"

"I loved to explore the country on foot," Frank said. "Going to visit them was exciting."

"Exciting? Wasn't it dangerous?"

"I suppose sometimes it was. But we were confident we would be fine, even when an elegant Arab man got off the bus with us."

His golden brown robe showed he was special. A large entourage of people, including women, encircled him. They all walked together speaking a mixture of Arabic and Hebrew. Within the next 30 minutes, moving his hand from left to right, the Arab man explained that all the land we could see belonged to him.

Once more I had to ask, "Weren't you scared?"

"No," Frank said. "I remember when I was a little boy Jews and Arabs often were nice to one another."

As they continued their walk down a one-lane sandy road, the Earth evolved to brilliant reddish brown. "I recall thinking, this is good earth," Frank said. "We are lucky to walk here with such a pleasant group."

On the left side of the road were large orange groves. At one point, when they were about to part ways, the Arab put his fingers into his mouth and gave a loud whistle. Four people emerged from the orange trees. They carried fruit nestled in the bottom of their shirts. This was the Arab's gift to Frank and his family, a special token of friendship.

"I loved the oranges and wanted to be able to buy one from a market whenever I was hungry," Frank said. "I felt the urge to earn my own money bubble up again. But I was a kid. What could I do?"

From time to time Frank's father brought a newspaper home from Tel Aviv. After his father and grandfather read it, Frank delivered the used newspaper to a neighbor who gave him a few mils—a few cents. It wasn't enough. What else could he do?

Frank thought about his problem later as he was flying his kite.

"I liked to race kites with friends," Frank said. "There were such wonderful winds coming in from the sea. Early in the morning I would secure my kite near the door and let it fly all day while I was in school. Other boys did the same. When I returned, my kite would still be in the air. It felt good because I had made the kite myself."

"No wonder you're such an expert at making kites for all the grandchildren," I said remembering pink, blue and yellow tissue paper kites flying over our local beach.

"I didn't just make them," Frank said. "As a kid I used to participate in kite competitions. I tied razor blades to the string then flew them over a field. The goal was to maneuver the kites so that my razor would cut the opponent's string, causing his kite to fly loosely and land far away. If my kite was cut, I ran to the hills to retrieve it. Of course the kites still flying won."

"Who gave you a razor?" I asked.

"I don't remember," he said. "Maybe I borrowed it from my father's shaving things. He didn't ask. I didn't discuss it."

Frank's grandfather watched the competitions and suggested he start a kite-making business.

"Everyone lived off the land in those days," Frank said. "So I cut the bamboo that grew in the sand near our house. It was perfect for kite frames."

His grandfather contributed colorful tissue and string and made glue out of a mixture of flour and water. Frank hired his sister to knot the kite tails out of thin strips of white paper. Chezzi's father, who managed Mr. Eckman's general store in Tel Aviv, agreed to sell them for him.

"I made over ten kites a week and earned enough money to buy whatever I wanted," Frank said. "It was easy because I didn't want much. Besides, I was enjoying the entrepreneurial process as much as the profits."

11: Choices Count

*1944   Despite the reversal in its fortunes of war, Germany
increases deportation and extermination of Jews,
with an estimated 1.3 million at Auschwitz alone.*

*Dr. Carl Joseph and his wife, Bette, are gassed in
Auschwitz.*

"I loved my life in Bat Yam," Frank said. "By the time I
was 10 or 11, I could switch from German at home to
Hebrew at school without noticing the difference. I even
picked up a smattering of Arabic."

His parents had a more challenging experience.
Although they attended classes at night, they struggled to
understand Hebrew and Arabic—the two languages they
needed to function efficiently in the Middle East.
Sometimes Hilda and Fritz stepped out to dinner with their
Arab classmates who lived in Jaffa and also wanted to
study Hebrew.

"My parents told me the Arabs worried their culture
and way of life were being eroded by the continuous influx
of immigrants," Frank said. "German naval submarines
were stationed off the coast of Jaffa. My parents' new

friends also shared rumors that Arab fishermen were informing the Germans where to find Jewish homes and important buildings."

Although Frank's parents and their Arab classmates felt warmth toward each other, political lines were being drawn. The Arabs had their viewpoint and the Jews had theirs. Each group followed its own agenda. No matter what friendships were blooming, every person was automatically on one side or the other. In between were the British.

"The war was expanding. Crime was growing and, due to our isolated location, my father agreed to get a dog," Frank said. "We bought a purebred black and gold German Shepherd named Kushy. She was our protector. I trained her to carry the mail in her mouth from the post office. She was my friend and followed me to the sea to swim."

Frank's folks believed an animal had to live its natural life, meaning that a female dog should give birth to puppies. Since their dog was a purebred, they asked around until they found another pure German Shepherd. Kushy produced a litter of ten puppies.

"We kept the puppies for six months," Frank said, "even though they ate our chickens and scared everyone with their barking."

Feeding so many animals was expensive. There were no supermarkets where one could buy dog food.

"My *opi* walked to the butcher and small markets to get scraps of meat and bones," Frank said.

Friends and relatives were afraid of the dogs and didn't like to visit. As the pets grew bigger, the problems got bigger so the family gave some of the puppies away, one to the dog's father and two to a kibbutz called Alonim in the north in Lower Galilee where a distant relative lived and cared for sheep. The British army bought the remaining seven puppies to train for military purposes.

"It felt odd knowing our dogs might sniff out illegal immigrants, good people who were trying to become part of our country," Frank said. "I was told the dogs were taught to find land mines that might be buried in strategic dividing points between the Jews and the Arabs. I don't know if the mines really existed. I never heard of any exploding. However, I was very proud that our dogs might help save people from such a disaster."

By now Frank and his family had been in the Middle East for many years. They still used their thin German white porcelain dishes even when they sat outside on their porch for breakfast. They used chrome clips to secure a tablecloth against the desert breeze and they ate grapefruits and oranges, the fruit of their new land, with toasted bread and homemade orange marmalade.

"Just like I picture my family did in Berlin," Frank said.

Arab traders often came by with fruits and vegetables in wooden boxes strapped to each side of their donkeys. "*Maranzes*," they yelled. Jewish women invited the merchants into their homes to spread their oranges on the floor. Each woman then selected the ones she wanted— 10 oranges for the equivalent of 20 cents.

"My favorite peddler was Sliman," Frank said. "One day he stopped coming around. When he returned, he said he had suffered from a sugar disease, which meant he was selling sugar illegally and might have been in prison."

On a particular weekend in 1944, two Arabs walked in front of the Levy balcony. They were dressed in their usual loose pants tied tightly at the ankles. Their skin was darker and they did not wear shoes.

"Somehow, I managed to understand a bit of the Arabic they were speaking," Frank said. "Their discussion revolved around which one of them would get our house when the German army marched into Palestine."

Germany was annexing land and German Field Marshal Erwin Rommel was marching his troops and tanks up the coast of North Africa. Once again, WWII was closing in on them.

"Every night my sister and I went to bed with a backpack at our feet. It contained bread, cans of food and a change of clothes," Frank said. "We never knew if we might have to flee with our backpacks to the dunes or to the North."

"American Colonel Paul W. Tibbets, who was a commander at the time, supported the Allied invasion in North Africa and led the first B-17 bombing raids after the initial invasion called Operation Torch," Frank said. "Maybe he helped stop Rommel. Maybe he saved my life."

In 1945 Tibbets became the commander and pilot of the Enola Gay, the plane that carried the atomic bomb dropped on Hiroshima.

In 1995, to commemorate the 50-year anniversary of the end of WWII, many of the original crew joined Colonel Tibbets to co-sign a limited edition fine art print of the Enola Gay that was published by The Greenwich Workshop in Connecticut. The crew also was filmed for a video screened at the Smithsonian National Air and Space Museum in Washington, D.C. The Greenwich Workshop asked me to work with them to help train Colonel Paul W. Tibbets for interviews with the media.

My first reaction was to say no. I did not want to be in the middle of emotional demonstrations between American war veterans and anti-war groups who were against the bombing of Japan. Frank never interfered with my work but this time he coaxed me to accept the assignment. It was an opportunity to integrate my life with a small part of his past. Thanks to Frank's encouragement, I met with Colonel Tibbets, Dutch Van Kirk and many other members of the crew.

After visiting Wendover Air Force Base in Utah where the squadron had been trained and where I caught up on WWII historical details, I began to understand Frank's life a little bit better. Later Frank joined me at the United States Air Force 509th Composite Group 50-year reunion in Arizona.

I started to read more history books. But I couldn't understand how my husband felt safe during the1940s wearing a dog tag with his name and relatives' names so that his parents could find him should he get swept up in some violent maelstrom.

"You have to understand," Frank said. "I did feel safe. I had my family and friends. We stuck to a routine. My parents were concerned when I took the local bus to kibbutz Alonim to help plant the land and tend the sheep, but not because I went alone. They wanted me to be highly educated in the German way. They worried I would quit school to become a farmer. My country was growing and I loved it and I did want to work the land. Despite the stories my folks told about their motherland and the war that was raging across Europe, even despite my backpack at the foot of my bed, all I really knew was a simple, happy life."

In 1944 the International Red Cross notified Frank's grandmother, Marta Jacobson, that her brother, Dr. Carl Joseph, and his wife, Bette, had been killed in Auschwitz in Germany. Their choice to stay in Berlin had cost them their lives.

"How did the Red Cross find your family?" I asked. "They could have been living anywhere in the world."

"The Germans kept precise records," Frank said. "Remember Theresienstadt?"

"Of course I remember," I said.

On our second trip to Czechoslovakia, after it had become a free capitalist country, I decided to visit the Theresienstadt Concentration Camp. Frank didn't want that experience. When I considered going alone, of course he joined me. We're both like that, always doing things together.

We hired a taxi to drive us from Prague to Terezin where the camp is located. I can never forget the exhibits of metal spikes the Nazis wore on their boots to kick inmates who were too weak to work. Sometimes when I see photos of German Shepherds, what plays in my mind is how the dogs must have nipped the prisoners. I can never erase the vision of the room in which we stood, the same room where thousands of people had been crowded together, starving, sick, working until they fell, perhaps to be shot and then cremated.

We entered under a huge sign, *Arbeit Macht Frei:* Work Makes you Free. In 1942 Dr. Joseph and Bette had entered under that sign and I could imagine the world closing in on them.

Along a path we discovered a tunnel.

"It's too sinister for me," I said. "Don't go in. It's where they shot prisoners."

Frank walked in anyway. Minutes passed. Other tourists emerged, but no Frank. I stepped into the entrance and was immediately engulfed by the dark.

"Frank," I yelled. An echo was my only answer. I backed out to the sunshine. Eventually Frank emerged in tears.

"The tunnel got narrower and narrower," he said. "I heard voices, probably other visitors returning from the end of the passageway. My imagination was active and I got scared."

Before we left the camp we asked a guard if we could view a list of inmates. She pointed to a stark building nearby. Inside, the semi-gloss white walls reminded me of a hospital. We pulled on tall, thick black iron doors. They were locked. The halls on both sides of the gate were empty. I pushed a buzzer on the wall and waited. A female voice blasted from some unseen place.

"Can we help you? What do you want?" the voice said. The words were in Czech then repeated in English.

"We think our relatives were here," Frank said, remembering the message the Red Cross had sent to his family in Bat Yam. "Is there a record of what happened to them?"

The voice said nothing but the doors inched open. Reluctantly, I followed Frank inside. Bang, the doors slammed shut, locking us in. In contrast, a cheery woman in a business suit appeared from a side room to welcome us into her office. Frank told her about his uncle and the dates of his internment. It took the woman about 60 seconds, maybe less, to pull a binder off a white shelf. The binder contained names, dates and numbers of inmates. Dr. Joseph was listed in that first book she had grabbed.

"Yes," she said. "They were here from 1942 to 1944. They came with a small group from Berlin."

"And then?" I asked noticing her smile had disappeared.

"Then they were transported with thousands of others to Auschwitz," she said.

"Should we assume they were among those sent to the ovens?" I asked.

"I am sorry," she said in English with her thick Czech accent. Her words sounded as emotional as please pass the salt.

Frank thanked her for her time. He thanked her!! He told her she was helpful. He appreciated her efforts. *Cold bitch* was about to roll off my tongue, but I kept quiet. *Just doing her job*, I thought. *Just like the Nazis.*

Our ride back to Prague was silent.

12: Rescued From Darkness

1942 Colonel Paul W. Tibbets bombs North Africa.

*1944 British Mandate further restricts Jewish immigrants
to Palestine.*

"Would I ever see again? I wanted to ask, but was too
afraid to hear the answer," Frank said. Both his eyes were
bandaged and he was ordered to stay in a dark room
without moving. He was only 11 and felt this was too big a
punishment for his simple prank.

Just a few days before, Frank had crossed from
Jewish Bat Yam into Arab Jaffa where the two cities
merged. On the Bat Yam side was a six-story beer factory
that overshadowed the small houses near the beach. On the
Jaffa side were fields with sparse low plants and beautiful
cacti flowers that had prickly pears—sabras—like the
nickname for modern day Israeli soldiers or those born in
Israel, sweet on the inside, prickly and tough on the
outside.

The Arabs let their donkeys graze in these fields.
During the day, the animals served as the major
transportation for merchants to carry fruits and vegetables

they were selling. In the late afternoon after work, there could be 20 to 30 donkeys munching on whatever greenery they might find.

"I already had ridden my *abba*'s horses that pulled his bakery buggies in Tel Aviv so I knew I could ride a donkey," Frank said. "It was so tempting."

He convinced two friends to join him after school. They raced to the field and when nobody was looking, hopped onto the donkeys and rode up and down the area.

"Bareback?" I asked.

"Of course bareback and without reins," Frank said. "To move, we yelled '*dio*' and to stop we yelled '*hoish*.' Although these were Hebrew commands, somehow they worked just fine with the Arab donkeys. I didn't realize this bit of fun would be the start of the two worst weeks of my life."

A few days after the donkey escapade, Frank's *opi* noticed his eyes were red. The next day they were redder. His grandson had some sort of inflammation. Hilda and Fritz were both at work. *Opi* was so concerned he immediately took Frank on a bus north of Tel Aviv to an eye doctor.

"You have to understand," Frank said. "This was not so simple. First we walked about half a mile along an extremely hot, sandy road to the local bus stop where we waited for an unscheduled bus, hoping one would come soon."

On the half hour ride to Tel Aviv they chatted with friends and neighbors going in the same direction. The bus station in Tel Aviv was much bigger, a gathering depot for all the buses from smaller towns. The confusion of many people from different backgrounds added to Frank's anxiety until they caught the right bus to the eye doctor.

Soon enough he learned he had contracted Trachoma, an eye disease prevalent in the Middle East at that time. It could cause blindness if not treated without delay. Frank's case was severe on both the upper and lower lids so the doctor operated on him right then.

"I still can feel the injections that numbed the area on each side of my eyes," he said. "I can hear the scraping of the knife removing residue from the infection."

After both eyes were bandaged they took the bus back to Tel Aviv, then a second bus to Bat Yam before walking the half-mile to their house. This time Frank was in total darkness, holding onto his grandfather who guided him along the road one slow step after the next, the entire way home.

The doctor had ordered him to stay in the dark without moving his head. Normally Frank slept on the living room couch that opened to a bed. It was in the sunniest area next to their light wood bookcases and modern Bauhaus style furniture developed in Berlin. His parents gave him their room because they could clamp down the windows and close the heavy shutters over the door, providing the dark environment he needed.

"I felt terrible that everyone was inconvenienced because of me. The worst was the terror of losing my eyesight. It was stronger than my fear every time I heard air raid sirens warning us to hide from possible bombs heading for Tel Aviv just six kilometers away."

At those moments every family took in strangers who happened to be walking by. Today most houses in Israel have bomb shelters. Back then people huddled inside the concrete hallway between the kitchen and bathroom waiting for the danger to pass.

"It was chilling," Frank said.

The whole community also experienced the same health concerns about bacterial infections and other easily transmitted diseases that were prevalent in the Middle East during those years. Frank was taught to wash his hands after he touched the rabbits or chickens. His *omi* put potassium permanganate crystals into water, making it turn purple. They soaked their fruits and vegetables for 30 minutes in this colorful mixture then washed off the chemicals along with any remaining bacteria.

"Sharing such precautions with my family was comforting," Frank said. "Nearly everyone was displaced, starting over, figuring out how to survive. I felt reassured, knowing my worries matched those of the whole neighborhood. My fear while my eyes were bandaged was all mine."

Flat on his back, Frank was treated with extra favorite foods. For Shabbat his grandmother prepared bread then brought it to a local bakery to bake it for her. This was part of their Friday ritual, enabling them to enjoy the delicious braided challah. For two weeks Frank got a little more.

Before his eye operation Frank had done his homework in the living room on a huge piece of furniture that looked like a paneled box. When he opened the top cover, it turned into a desk. On each side were glass-fronted cabinets where the family kept books and photo albums. Most books were in German. There was a complete set of Shakespeare in English as well as the beginning of a collection of books in Hebrew.

"But I couldn't do any homework," Frank said. "I was surprised how much I missed the routine."

Though Ada was five, usually she still slept in her parents' room. Both Ada's and her parents' beds were made out of painted tubular steel frames—theirs green and hers white. Her steel frame was too difficult to move so while Frank recuperated she slept on the floor in the living room.

After school Ada loved to visit her girlfriend from Yemen who lived in a concrete building that had no windows or doors. In the center of the main room they cooked on a fire on the sand floor. Their family was very poor, but there was a special warmth that attracted Ada and her mother always knew where to find her at the end of the day.

"Even my little sister was too busy for me," Frank said.

Their dog, Kushy, slept outside at night, only allowed inside during the day.

"I really missed running and tossing a ball for her to catch. I couldn't swim in the sea with her or take her on walks to purchase our daily food."

"In Bat Yam, one day was the same as the next," Frank said. "Time seemed to move slowly—school, lunch, a rest from the unbearable heat in midday and then after dinner, time with friends. But when I was confined to bed, time didn't move at all. I was stuck, scared and full of energy with nothing to do."

There were no phones in the house, so the only connection with people outside family and nearby friends was the post office. But of course Frank couldn't go there. He was trapped in his parents' bed with pillows keeping his head still in 24-hours of darkness day after day after day. He could hear his mother tiptoeing in and out, but since Trachoma is highly contagious, no friends were allowed to visit.

Frank wasn't used to such isolation. Despite different religious and political groups living near each other, the area was so safe he was allowed to take trips with his friends to other cities. Nobody worried a child might be abducted or molested. Now he couldn't go with his friends. He couldn't accompany his grandfather to the Arab *souk* in Jaffa, a place Frank thought was more exciting than any other outdoor market he encountered. Instead he lay bandaged and motionless, quiet for hours and hours.

"No books. No company. Nothing," Frank said.

That's when his *Opi* filled Frank's days with tales of ice sailing on the frozen lake in Crivitz, Germany, of tying a sheet and holding it up to the wind.

"It sounded magical," Frank said. "I knew I would visit one day."

Opi described their brick house and peaceful town where he grew up. He told Frank about the synagogue, the family department store and all the people who once lived above the store while employed below.

"I loved my grandparents," Frank said, "but mostly I loved my grandfather. He made Crivitz so real that when I traveled there 40 years later, I knew exactly where to walk to find my grandfather's house."

After two dreadful weeks, Frank and his *opi* took the unscheduled local bus back to Tel Aviv. *Opi* held Frank's hand and led him, sightless, to his seat.

"I tried to figure out where we were and when we turned right or left and how long the ride would be," Frank said. "I tried to think of anything to get my mind off the next hour. I couldn't help but wonder what my life would be like if I could never have my vision back."

The doctor took off his bandages right away, but Frank was afraid to open his eyes. The lids seemed to be stuck. What if he couldn't see?

"I was incredibly relieved to be able to look at the doctor's face," Frank said. "His glasses that magnified his brown eyes, his rosy cheeks and his miraculous smile will forever be branded in my memory. The doctor also built model airplanes that were so big a grown up could sit inside. Once my eyes focused, he took me to his workshop to see his planes."

Back home, Frank walked through the long, wide hallway that connected the rooms. He loved being able to look at the familiar old dark wooden German Grandfather Clock and green storage cabinets. On top was a wooden crate that contained white sugar cubes to be opened and tasted when the war ended. Frank and his sister had never tasted plain sugar. He tried to convince his parents to give him some in celebration of his rescue from darkness. They insisted he wait.

"I was sorry I had ridden the Arabs' donkeys without permission," Frank said. "I'll never know if I caught Trachoma from those donkeys or if it already was in my system from our rabbits and chickens.

Either way, since I was rescued from blindness, I promised myself I'd behave and follow all the rules at school and at home, which I did... for the next few months."

13: The War Is Over

1945 April 30: Hitler commits suicide.

May 8: WWII ends in Europe. Frank Levy tastes his first sugar cube.

August 5: U.S. drops atomic bomb on Japan.

"Didn't you celebrate the end of the war?" I asked, thinking about the photos of parades in America and reading about the good cheer that filled everyone with relief and joy.

"I would like to say I was excited, but to tell you the truth, I don't remember any of it," Frank said. "Maybe my parents listened to the BBC on our radio. They knew some English and were always listening to the BBC. I know we opened the sugar cubes. Some had ants so we threw those away. The others we shared. I had waited so long to taste sugar. When I did, I much preferred the chocolate soup my mother used to make for me on my birthday."

"Did your parents consider returning to Germany?" I asked.

"My parents were determined to unite with Uncle Herbert." Frank said. "Besides, Europe was such a disaster

65

most people didn't want to live in what might have been left of their old homes even if they could."

Frank's mother always told him to learn from the past, but not go back. Perhaps she understood that their little Hermsdorf neighborhood would become part of East Berlin and be taken over by the communists. She taught her son that no matter what happened, it was the future he must look to if he were to fulfill his dreams.

Shortly after the war ended, Frank's *abba* took him on a special trip.

"Just the two of us," Frank said. "Our car had been confiscated by the British quite some time before so we took a bus to Tel Aviv, a train north to Haifa and then another bus to *Safed*, the highest city in Galilee."

"That's a center for *Kaballah*, right" I asked.

"If you say so," Frank said.

"Those who follow the mystical prayers often wear a red string on their left wrists for spiritual and physical protection and blessings," I said, thinking of Madonna and other celebrities I'd read about in magazines while getting a manicure.

On the way Frank and his *abba* had stopped at kibbutz Alonim to visit Kushy's puppies. At the time Frank didn't know the trip was part of saying goodbye to all of their friends and family and land. He was thrilled to stay at a hotel where they met others who were going on the same hike—a group of ten adults and their children ready to picnic on one of the tallest mountains in the area. During the picnic, a group of Arabs on horses approached. They were not wearing uniforms, but they carried guns.

"They told us to leave," Frank said. "Now."

The picnickers packed up their food and grabbed their blanket.

"We didn't bother to fold it in good German style," Frank said. "We walked as fast as we could down the hill. The Arabs rode their horses behind us. They didn't say anything, but we heard the clomp of their horses' hoofs. We could feel how close they were. They didn't shoot. They didn't hurt the Jewish families, but I was terrified."

"Worse, I knew my fearless *abba* also was scared," Frank said.

Back in Haifa Frank and his father caught a train to the Tel Aviv train station at the outskirts of the city. In Tel Aviv the two were swallowed up by crowds rushing in all directions. Instead of grabbing Frank's hand to make sure they weren't separated, Fritz told Frank to rush ahead and get on line to catch a local bus to the main bus station. They needed to catch that bus in order to connect to another bus that would take them to Bat Yam. His father had wanted to be sure they would have seats.

"I could sense his urgency. In my haste I tripped over railroad tracks and gashed my head," Frank said, showing me his scar. "Fleeing from the Arabs, hurrying through the throng, falling out of control and realizing that my father was anxious had a tremendous impact, one I'll never forget. For the first time I began to feel that the land I loved was filled with danger."

14: Did They Know?

*1945 April: Soviets attack Berlin. Russian army
approaches Sachsenhausen Concentration Camp
near Crivitz, Germany.*

*April 21: Dr. Fritz Rohde views the Death March of
Jews evacuating the Sachsenhausen Concentration
Camp.*

Following are more excerpts from Dr. Fritz Rohde's diary.
He was 16 at the end of the war when the Sachsenhausen
Concentration Camp was emptied. Frank translated the
memoir out loud so both of us could digest the stories at the
same time.

> At the end of April 1945 I remember a
> British plane dropped bombs that hit the
> Catholic Church as well as a number of other
> buildings. There was so much shooting by the
> British that a whole column of trucks was
> destroyed. I counted at least 30 trucks that
> were shot up. A friend of mine was working

with his dad in a bicycle repair shop. They were killed.

On another corner I saw a light painted bus that was bombed out. All the windows were broken. The seats were torn. There was blood all over. The bus had a big red cross on it and two nurses were in the bus, dead. The townspeople buried the nurses in our cemetery in the grave of the unknown soldiers.

Soon after, Crivitz was filled with foreigners. There were poorly-dressed soldiers from Romania, and others maybe from Italy. Their officers stood by in good uniforms. Day by day, every morning until night, we saw Nazis who looked for women.

On May 1, 1945, it was a sunny day after a very cold night. In my house in the morning I heard a very strange noise. It was a melancholy shuffling that would not stop. In the beginning I believed this noise to be the result of a number of track-driven vehicles like tanks coming our way. Of course, we hoped the Americans were coming to our city before the Russians came, but the Americans already had passed through Crivitz. Our Mayor, Han, had been seen in an American Jeep with a white flag.

To see what was causing this awful noise, I walked to the Parchimerstrasse where the Jacobson store stood.

Frank stopped reading to process the fact that the store mentioned was his grandfather's store. A moment later he continued translating.

There I saw an awful scene—worse than awful—one that I shall never forget. So close, directly in front of me, was a sight that I have never before nor since been exposed to. I was confronted with such misery that hid itself behind the words "concentration camp."

In the middle of this human escaping storm I saw groups of prisoners in their loose striped clothing, maybe 50-100 people per group, coming down a hill to Parchimerstrasse. They walked next to each other, supporting each other, dragging each other forward, slowly, without any energy, step by step, shuffling their feet in heavy wooden shoes. That was the noise I heard—thousands of wooden shoes moving on the hard cobblestone road. I could not even understand what I was witnessing.

Later I learned that the SS was clearing out the concentration camps in preparation for the arrival of the Russian and American troops. Two camps, KZ Sachsenhausen and KZ Ravensbruck, were just miles from Crivitz. Thousands of prisoners were marching 155 miles from the camps to Lubeck on the sea, perhaps to drown.

In contrast to these poor people stood the well-fed Nazi guards in uniform. They held wooden knuppels—fat police sticks—ready to hit. I remember so well that the guards who were forcing the prisoners to keep moving wore extra good uniforms with red bandanas around their necks.

It was clear that the Nazis had dragged many people. Some of them were Jehovah's Witnesses. This group was originally from

Hamburg, but their Nazi officer was from Crivitz.

As a group of prisoners inched past me, I did not see the expected fright and shock because their big dark eyes seemed burned out without any reactions. Then I realized they were women in prison garments—the clothing of punishment. It was so awful to see the effects of starvation, especially when compared to the well-fed guards. It was hard to tell the ages of the people. They were very thin in their striped clothing. Their faces were gray. The prisoners seemed not to notice the Crivitz people staring at them from the edge of the street. The women could barely move forward.

In between, however, I saw women who had some strength supporting the weaker ones in order to keep the group together. They did not want to give up and did not want to give in. They did not want to fall down because, for sure, falling down would be the end. I realized they were determined to reach their goal—freedom—they did not want to give up. It was clear they thought freedom could not be too far away.

The image of these women who had gone through the hell of a concentration camp and who still kept their pride has stayed with me all these years. I feel the responsibility to humanity to remember just these women and to report about them so that they never will be forgotten. In our cemetery in Crivitz there is a memorial to the people of the death march from KZ Sachsenhausen.

Frank paused again. I could see he was filled with so many different emotions.

Such death marches existed like a net all over Germany. I'm only describing what I saw. At night the prisoners were sent into the woods to make camp. According to history books, around May 6 thousands of these prisoners were rescued by the second Belarussion front and by American troops. The prisoners from KZ Sachsenhausen spent their last night in captivity in the woods in Crivitz. When they were liberated, it is said that some guards put on the prisoners' clothes to save their own lives.

Russian soldiers came next, in all kinds of military trucks, as well as on foot. They did a lot of shooting. We hid in a corner of our cellar with our mother. We were scared and held onto each other while mother prayed. For years we could see the bullet holes on many buildings in town.

15: Coming Of Age, 1946

1946 RCA manufactures the first mass produced television.

United Nations Security Council holds its first meeting.

Oct. 24: First trial of Nazi war criminals in Nuremberg.

"1946 was very special," Frank said. "I was turning 13, about to celebrate my bar mitzvah along with all my classmates."

Frank had attended school with the same children since he was six. They stayed together from class to class and year to year, becoming an extended family. Only the teachers changed.

September was just two months before his big birthday and he was very excited. Soon he would be counted as a man, officially coming of age. As he practiced his section of the Torah to read at his bar mitzvah, he dreamed of getting the school gift that was given to each boy on this momentous occasion—a plaster bust of Theodor Herzl.

"I still remember my *abba* explaining that Herzl was the founder of Zionism, dedicated to forming a separate Jewish state."

"You were excited to get a plaster bust of a hero?" I asked. "I can't imagine an American boy wanting a plaster head of anyone."

Frank smiled.

"You have to understand," he said. "I also looked forward to my birthday because as a teen, I could participate in some of the more meaningful but dangerous political activities."

Although WWII was over, refugees were still flooding into the country and Palestine was in turmoil with different militant and diplomatic groups attempting to oust the British and form a Jewish state.

"I had come so far since joining my school in 1939 that I already felt grown up. I remember my disappointment when I couldn't sit on the same bench next to Avia because she was a girl. To get her attention, I caught a fly and tied a string from my sweater to its leg."

"*That's impossible*," I thought then changed my mind, picturing summers in the Hamptons, sitting outside on our deck watching Frank catch any fly that dared to stray near his hands.

I think flies were bigger in Bat Yam," he said. "I was able to dip the string into my inkwell and send it toward Avia. The fly flew all over, but never to her. It landed on other kids' heads and clothes, spreading ink from the yarn. The next day I had to bring my *ema* to school."

Another time Frank was reprimanded because his head was uncovered in religious school. He had worn a navy blue French beret to class. At home his *abba* and he did not wear a skullcap. Frank didn't like wearing one at school. When he took off his beret, the teacher yelled at him in front of the class for having a bare head. He flung his cap at her, Frisbee style, surprised that it smacked her right in the face.

"The next day I had to bring my *ema* to school again," Frank said.

"So you weren't always so sweet."

Frank smiled his Cheshire smile.

Outside of school he and his friends had much more freedom and fun. They loved playing soccer. During ten-minute intermissions between classes his group held continuous games that lasted the entire school year. Since they did not have enough money to own a real soccer ball, Frank made one from his mother's torn stockings and old clothes. It was good enough.

"Still, I dreamed that one of my bar mitzvah presents would be a real soccer ball," he said. "And maybe even a bicycle with lights."

When WWII ended, Zionist groups became more active, trying to establish an independent Jewish state. Some were extremely militant. On July 22, 1946, the radical group, *Irgun*, took credit for blowing up a wing of the King David Hotel in Jerusalem where the British Palestine Command was stationed. This attack killed British, Arab and Jewish people and set off some very tough days. Political violence was not the only safety problem. It was a primitive time and Bat Yam, squeezed between the desert, the sea and Jaffa, endured many robberies.

The little police station was on the second floor over a vegetable store. Very few people worked there.

"It was said the town had only one gun and one telephone at the police station," Frank said. "Citizens were unprotected, so my *abba* and other men in the village formed *Haga*, a civil defense group that took turns watching town in two-to-four hour shifts at night. My parents wouldn't let me take a shift. So I joined the *HaNoar*

HaOved, a working youth group. Through them I became devoted to social equality."

What ensued was a philosophical rift at home. Frank's parents were capitalists who still yearned for concerts, fancy sweet cakes and the more formal lifestyle they had left in Germany. The only reason they had joined the *Haga* was to defend themselves. When they worked the land, it was to survive.

"My friends and I believed in working the land we loved," Frank said. "I learned more about heroes like Herzl and Jabotinsky who believed in establishing an independent state. I read about Trumpeldor, the early Zionist activist who died in 1920, saying, 'It is good to die for one's country.' I was caught up in the movement and Zionism became important to me."

Frank's friend Chezzi would not join any of the youth groups. Perhaps that's why he was selected by his school to welcome the first trainload of orphans who had survived the Holocaust.

"It must have made quite an impact," Frank said, "because when he grew up, Chezzi became a psychoanalyst and childcare worker at a residential treatment center. Later he was named the director and voted in as president of the Israeli Psychoanalytic Society."

During this turbulent time social equality in the British Mandate gave birth to kibbutzim. Frank loved visiting these collective farms that were organized to build the land while providing separate communities for people to live and work. Sometimes he helped herd sheep early in the morning. Sometimes he picked grapes and put them into wooden boxes strapped to donkeys. At kibbutz Alonim, adults, teens and children danced and sang songs that made them feel united. The words carried messages about the land and friendship and the importance of all for one and one for all.

"It felt so good to belong," Frank said.

Meanwhile, as Frank studied the portion of the Torah to read for his bar mitzvah, his parents planned a big trip for the family.

"We were going to the United States to visit Uncle Herbert," Frank said, "and my cousins, Laurel and Beryl, whom I had never met, and my other grandmother, Alice."

The evening before his departure, Frank was promised this was only a vacation. Otherwise his friends would have found a way to hide him and he would have stayed behind. Everyone knew that his friend Patch had jumped off a ship in the Haifa Harbor as it sailed the rest of his family back to Hungary after the war. Everyone knew that with a little planning, it was possible for a kid to remain in Palestine.

Frank didn't worry about his dog because Kushy stayed behind with his grandparents, but he had a premonition when his grandfather gave him a watch and a small olive wooden box.

"Why should I get a good watch just to go on holiday? When I saw my sister take her special doll," Frank said, "I grabbed my little black wooden dog that I had brought from Venice."

Though he went with his parents, in his heart he realized this was no vacation. Somehow he knew that in two weeks he was not going to be keeping his plans with Chezzi.

"I felt that if I were to return to Palestine, it would be well into the future, on my own," Frank said. He wasn't wrong.

At the airport Hilda and Fritz stuffed a big duffle bag containing extra large down bedding and a few belongings into a small two-engine airplane in Lod, the only airport in the area outside of Tel Aviv. They also carried a small Persian carpet, a red leather purse and a few other gifts for Aunt Stella and Uncle Herbert. The oversized bag had to be pushed by three people and barely fit into the narrow luggage compartment.

Wearing his customary short khaki pants and brown leather sandals, Frank and his family boarded a small two-engine plane to Cairo to meet a bigger aircraft to New York. The small plane held seven people, counting the four of them. It was Frank's first flight.

"We lifted off and the plane rattled and roared. It made more noise than radio static and shouts on the buses and air raid sirens all put together," Frank said. "As I looked out the window flying south along the Mediterranean, I could see the areas that were so dear to me. There was Jaffa and there was Bat Yam. There were the large rocks that we jumped from to go for a swim. I even thought I could see our house where we had lived peacefully while the rest of the world endured political and economic turmoil."

They landed in Cairo, Egypt, where they waited for an unscheduled TWA plane to arrive. During the day they explored museums, pyramids, the Great Sphinx of Giza and other sites. They stayed at a simple hotel and visited the more opulent Mena House Hotel to swim in its marble pool.

"We could see the pyramids while swimming. We even had afternoon coffee at Café Groppi of Cairo in Suleiman Pasha Street, a famous spot. I remember it so vividly because that is where I tasted my first ice cream," Frank said, "peach flavored, served in a tall fluted glass topped with whipped cream."

And they waited. Finally, a week later, they left Egypt to start a 44-hour flight with stops in Algiers, Tunis, Madrid, Lisbon, Shannon, Newfoundland, Boston and New York. If he had stayed back, in two months Frank would have been one of the boys helping refugees sneak into the country. In two months, he would have received his plaster bust of Herzl. Instead, his parents forced him to abandon the camaraderie and dreams of his youth.

Frank had to give up the only homeland he knew. He gave up his friends, his devotion to protect the environment, to build the land and his entire way of thinking to fulfill Grandma Alice's dream to unite the family.

"I hardly knew my relatives in America," Frank said. "It was not my choice."

"Your *kumbayah* moments were over," I said. "Weren't you angry?"

"It's not so simple," Frank said. "Whom should I be angry at? My parents didn't create the Nazis or the violence in Palestine. They didn't separate my father and Uncle Herbert. My parents taught me to look forward and that is what I had to do."

On the plane between Boston and New York City, Frank and his sister were offered black water. They were very thirsty, but couldn't put the bubbly liquid into their mouths.

"We had never seen Coca-Cola," Frank said. "It looked disgusting. But that was nothing compared to what came next. In Palestine I was called Yaakov. My mother told me that in America my father would be called Fred and I would be called Frank, the first name on my birth certificate."

If he had to change his name, Frank would have preferred Jack because it was similar to Jacob or Yaakov. But Uncle Herbert's brother-in-law, Aunt Stella's brother, was called Jack and the family didn't want any confusion.

Again, Frank would not understand the language spoken. He vowed that from then forward, he would make the important decisions in his life, not his parents.

"This time I was determined to conquer whatever came next on my own terms," Frank said. "I just wasn't sure what that meant."

Grandma Alice Levy reunited
her family in America.

Grandma Marta Jacobson &
Grandpa Martin Jacobson in Berlin,
Germany, 1930.

Fritz, Frank & Hilda Levy in Berlin, 1936.

Saturday afternoom coffee, 1935:
Hilda announced she and her family were leaving Berlin, Germany.
L to R: Bette & Dr. Carl Joseph (later killed in Auschwitz), Marta & Martin Jacobson,
Alice Levy, Hilda Levy & Hilda's Uncle Lulu Jacobson.

Hilda, Frank & Fritz Levy
leaving Europe on the S.S. Palestina, 1936.

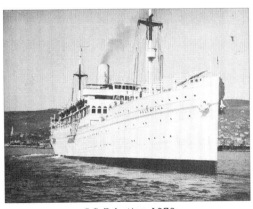

S.S. Palestina, 1936.
Sailing from Trieste, Italy to Jaffa, Palestine.

Ada & Frank
in Bat Yam.

Frank & a friendly Arab riding a donkey.

Frank feeding chickens in Kfar Sirkin.

Chezzi & Frank in Bat Yam.

Frank, Ada, Grandpa Martin,
Grandma Marta
& Frank's father, Fred,
in Bat Yam prior to the British
confiscating their car.

Frank & Kushy.
Frank is wearing the
leather jacket
Grandma Alice
sent from America.

Chezzi & Miriam Cohen w/ Ada & Frank Levy on the beach in
Bat Yam. Adam's Rock can be seen in the back right, 1944.

Fred, Hilda, Frank & Ada's Palestinian citizenship papers, February 21st, 1939.

Sova Bakery, Tel Aviv.

Fred, Frank, Ada, & Hilda on their porch
prior to leaving the Middle East for the USA, 1946.

Part II
America 101
1946-1981

16: New School, New Everything

*1946   Nuremberg Trial of Nazi War Criminals in
Germany.*

First meeting of the United Nations.

*Perry Como sang "I'm Always Chasing Rainbows,"
Frank Sinatra sang "Full Moon and Empty Arms"
and Dinah Shore sang "Laughing on the Outside."*

*March 5: Winston Churchill delivers speech
declaring an Iron Curtain has descended across the
European continent.*

"When my parents told me I was going to school in
America, I wondered if I'd ever see my dog again," Frank
said.

A week earlier Aunt Stella had taken him to
Benjamin's, a boys' clothing store in New Rochelle, New
York, where she bought him his first pair of long pants.
They were brown corduroy and made a scraping sound
when he walked. She also picked out a green and brown
plaid shirt.

"In Bat Yam my clothes had been cotton khaki," Frank said. "I had never seen plaid before. In the store I still thought I was going home soon. I didn't understand why I needed new clothes that looked like a silly costume."

Then Frank remembered English lessons his parents had given him a few months earlier. They had hired an Australian woman to walk with Frank and his sister on the beach and teach them English.

"The lady read us a story about Peter Rabbit who sneaked into Mr. McGregor's garden. I thought McGregor was a very unusual name," Frank said. "The instructor taught us a song about a mulberry bush. I had never heard of a mulberry and after decades in America I've never had to use that word."

Frank was not happy in his new clothes or in his new land.

"I knew it would be bad as soon as we emerged from the plane at the airport. As we climbed down the stairs I recognized Uncle Herbert and assumed the other two women were my Aunt Stella and Grandma Alice watching us from behind a wire fence. Inside the building people in every color outfit grabbed luggage and moved through long lines to get their passports stamped. I couldn't read the signs in English, so I followed my parents, feeling younger and more vulnerable than my almost 13 years."

"Didn't you come through Ellis Island?" I asked. "That's where my grandparents entered the country from Russia in 1904—or maybe it was 1906."

"No, coming to America was not so easy after the war."

Frank's uncle had started the immigration request years earlier when Frank and his parents still lived in Tel Aviv. Uncle Herbert wrote to the United States Consulate for a visa for his brother and family to visit America. Copies of his letters show he listed his savings at American Express and Chase National Bank in New York. He also provided details about his earnings as a consulting engineer for the textile industry. He promised, in writing, that he would not allow his brother to become a public charge.

"How did your family plan to switch from temporary to permanent residence?" I asked.

"I don't know," Frank said. "I didn't even know we were going to America until the night before we left. I was so upset about leaving I never bothered to ask about anything."

Despite repeated attempts, Herbert couldn't get visas, so in 1945 he changed his strategy and requested permanent residence. By then Herbert was a naturalized American citizen. He and his brother-in-law, Jack, traveled to Washington, D.C., to meet with the Department of State and guarantee that if his older brother, Fritz, did not have a job in America, Herbert would take care of the family. The document Herbert signed enabled Fritz to get a visa at the American Consulate in Jerusalem and to breeze through customs upon arrival in America a year later.

Outside the airport Fritz and Herbert hugged for a long time. Then they dragged their luggage to Herbert's 1941 Buick.

"The two-toned gray automobile looked about the size of the kitchen in our house back home," Frank said.

The car was so big it could hold Hilda, Fred, Ada and Frank, in the back seat and Uncle Herbert, Aunt Stella and Grandma Alice in front. Their huge duffle, a carpet and other bags were crammed into the trunk.

Frank had met his grandmother Alice only twice: seven years before when she had visited Palestine on her way to join Herbert in the United States and in 1936 just prior to when Hilda and Fritz left Germany. Sometimes Grandma Alice had sent clothes that Frank never wore because they were too fancy or too warm for his life in the desert.

"When I looked at Grandma Alice's soft, plump body and black hair sprinkled with gray," Frank said, "I don't know why I imagined she would have gifts for us. But she didn't. I was disappointed."

Nonetheless, the family move to America had a lot to do with Grandma Alice. She'd written numerous letters to Frank's father asking him to come overseas and reunite the family. She described a wonderful country with religious freedom and different groups living together in peace. She mentioned opportunities to build careers and educate children. She spoke about music and art and an abundance of food and friends. Alice's brother, Alfred, had come to the States in 1917. She was determined to pull her two sons and their families together after the war. So there they were, like it or not, about to start over again.

The car was quiet as they drove north over the Whitestone Bridge to Westchester County. "I had never been in such a smooth, fast, clean car—or ridden on such a wide highway with so much traffic. While the adults spoke rapidly in German, my sister and I looked out the window at the New York skyline and the expanse of water in the Long Island Sound."

In less than an hour they arrived at Uncle Herbert's house on Rockingstone Avenue in Larchmont, about 20 miles north of the city. It was a dead-end street with big trees, bigger than any Frank had seen in Palestine.

"The house was so huge it had a separate room just for a car," Frank said, "maybe big enough for two."

They entered through the kitchen. The first things Frank noticed were the appliances. "The refrigerator was gigantic compared to our small refrigerator. On top of the counter, instead of a single-burner Primus, there was a real stove with many burners that lit up just by turning a knob. And the house had an oven!"

Frank's parents and sister stayed upstairs and shared a bathroom. Frank was downstairs on the main floor with a bed next to a table that held a Singer sewing machine.

"For the first time in my life I did not have to wait my turn to use a bathroom," Frank said. "This house had more bathrooms than all our rooms in Bat Yam."

"The water pipes back home had been outside, so the temperature of the shower water depended upon the weather and the sun. Here the pipes were somewhere in the walls, heated elsewhere in the house. When I showered, I was amazed I could control whether I got hot or cold water from the faucets. How was that possible?"

Everything was different: instead of handles, the doors were adorned with round doorknobs. The windows opened up and down instead of outward. Screens prevented flies from entering. There was no sand anywhere. The floors were wood, not stone.

"Oriental rugs felt lush under our feet. I took off my shoes to let my toes sink into the fiber and right away I could see that you could be rich in America. Nonetheless, a saying that was popular in Bat Yam floated through my head: It is better to be poor and barefoot in our motherland than to sit in palaces in other countries."

Soon everyone was hungry, so Grandma Alice made something special: peanut butter and jelly sandwiches. Frank's two cousins, Laurel, who was four, and Beryl, who was two, both seemed to like the sandwiches.

"White bread had no recognizable flavor," Frank said. "Bread should be thick, brown and hearty like in Germany or from the bakery in Bat Yam or pita like the falafel sandwiches we bought from the Arab trucks. Though I liked the taste of the inside of the sandwich, I couldn't swallow. The peanut butter kept sticking to the top of my mouth and I needed a drink."

Grandma Alice poured milk from a glass bottle with a section for heavy cream. It was delivered daily. At home, or what used to be home, Frank's milk came from an Arab merchant who took it from his cows and put it into stainless steel jugs tied to both sides of his donkey.

"We used to buy quarter liters that were poured directly into our pots," he said.

Aunt Stella was pregnant when Frank and his family arrived. She told Frank that as a special gift for him another cousin would join them in April.

"Interesting," Frank said. "But after a 44-hour flight all I really wanted was to go to sleep."

On Monday, following a breakfast of eggs and toast, Fred and Frank commuted by train to New York City with Uncle Herbert.

"I had trouble thinking my dad's name was Fred, not Fritz. It was easier to continue to call him *abba* like I did in Bat Yam. Besides, it was our first week and I still thought it was a vacation."

Frank imagined his experience on a modern train would be just like in Palestine with wooden benches and hikers or people traveling on holiday. Here most of the passengers were men in suits and ties sitting on upholstered seats. The last ten minutes were through a long dark tunnel, seemingly under the city, right to Grand Central Station.

"It occurred to me that the subterranean passages would make a wonderful bomb shelter," Frank said.

The station was enormous. Frank kept staring at the high ceiling as he walked in slow motion. At the exit his father took his hand to guide him out to the street where they were blasted by sounds of cars honking. People were rushing, pushing past, but Frank stalled to look up to the sky and see the unbelievably tall buildings that seemed to rise forever.

It was his second day in the States and he had never seen such a wide street with so many cars speeding by amidst so much congestion. He'd never seen a traffic light. When it turned green, his father pulled his hand and directed him toward the Lincoln Building, the neo-gothic landmark with a light brown marble lobby, intricate ceiling and chandeliers.

They entered the elevator and Frank checked the new watch his grandfather had given him. His stomach flipped up and down as they soared to the 40th floor. It took just 40 seconds to reach his uncle's consulting company, a textile business Herbert had started when he settled in America in 1939.

"Looking down from the office window," Frank said, "I saw people and cars. They seemed like tiny toys amid lots of miniscule yellow taxis."

The plan had been for Fred to work for Herbert who had studied textiles in Zurich and was a consultant helping textile factories become more efficient. Instead, Fred opened up Trans World Trading Company with someone who also had just arrived from Palestine. The new little company was headquartered in Herbert's office. They exported American-made business-to-business industrial products to Palestine and, later, to Israel. They bought and resold machinery for airplanes and ice cream factories in addition to other businesses.

They also supplied Kibbutz Gan Shmuel with evaporators to concentrate orange juice before the juice was shipped around the world. Frank's distant cousin, Gidi Elden, lived there and was in charge of engineering as well as of making the concentrated orange juice.

At noon Frank and Fred rode the elevator down for lunch. In the restaurant each person put a coin in a slot and out came a sandwich or a drink or chicken. It was the Horn & Hardart where each dish sat behind a glass window. For under a dollar they could enjoy a complete meal.

"My immediate new favorite was apple pie," Frank said. "The only sweets I knew were the cakes my other grandmother, Marta, had baked. With little money and no restaurants we always ate at home. I kept using my coins to buy more apple pie, surprised that my father let me eat three slices and nothing else for lunch. I knew why. It was the first time I had smiled since we'd landed in New York."

A few weeks after moving in with Uncle Herbert, Frank's family sublet an apartment on the fifth floor of a charming old building on North Chatsworth Avenue in Larchmont.

"I can't even describe how I felt," Frank said. "With our own apartment, for sure this was no vacation. I missed my dog and I missed my *opi*."

Frank's mother also was unhappy. They were near the train station and she could hear the rumbling and whistle blowing. While she fixed up their home, Frank started to get ready for his new school.

"In fact there was absolutely no way I could prepare myself for what was to come."

Aunt Stella picked up Frank and Ada in the morning. First she dropped his sister at her fourth grade class. Ada's teacher yelled at the girl for days, saying she was stupid because she couldn't catch on to anything in English. They put her back to third grade. In 1961 Ada earned a Master of Arts Degree in Basic Medical Sciences from Harvard University and a few years later a Ph.D. in Biochemistry from New York University, moving on to become a well-known research cell biologist and a specialist in Electron Microscopy.

After they left Ada at school Stella drove Frank to Mamaroneck Junior High School to enter the eighth grade. He was used to walking to school, maintaining some sort of independence. He didn't like being driven. He was uncomfortable in his plaid shirt and corduroy pants. The huge red brick building, about two football fields long and two stories high, was cold and uninviting—nothing like his eight-room school back home.

Inside kids assembled in an auditorium that was bigger than any room Frank had ever seen. Once Frank's parents had taken him to Tel Aviv to see a Charlie Chaplin film. Frank cried so much when Chaplin fell into a barrel his mother shuffled him out so he wouldn't disturb the other people. That big theater was nowhere near the size of the new school auditorium.

During assembly the class stood to pledge allegiance to the flag.

"When I refused," Frank said, "a teacher tried to convince me to get up. I shook my head no. 'I am from the British Mandate, Palestina,'" I said. 'As soon as I turn 18 and graduate from high school, I plan to go home to help build the land.' Of course I told her in Hebrew so she didn't understand. But she left me alone."

Following the pledge and some loudspeaker announcements that Frank didn't comprehend, he was given a schedule telling him where to report for each subject. The page was in English. He couldn't read it. The letters were different and everything was backwards, written from left to right. Another student pointed to explain what was happening, trying to help.

"I was shocked that I had to switch my classroom every hour," Frank said. "I kept thinking I wasn't understanding correctly. My first class was in room 110. My next class was in room 210. I looked on either side of 110 but there was no number 210. It was upstairs! Back home we didn't have a second floor. By the time I found my class I walked in late to a room full of strangers. I could hear my new brown corduroy pants making noise every time I moved my legs."

At the end of the day one boy motioned to Frank to wait for him at the front door. The boy ran to his house across the street from the school and returned with a dozen volumes of *The Encyclopedia Britannica*. Frank thought, *only in America*.

"My aunt was annoyed because I didn't rush to her car to go home," Frank said.

Day two was worse. Frank came to school a little early and walked by kids who were milling around.

"I didn't realize the school stayed locked until a bell rang at 8:25 a.m. I pushed through the crowd not knowing I was being inappropriate, not realizing the others were already standing in line. I tried to open the door, as I would have done in Bat Yam. A big kid, maybe even a senior who looked like he played ball, said something in English then punched me in the nose. I bled. A lot. My mother was summoned to school. Aunt Stella had to drive her and translate. They took me to a hospital in nearby New Rochelle with blood all over my new plaid shirt."

By day three Frank's parents hired an English tutor to work with him and his sister three afternoons a week. The "th" sound, as in Martha instead of Marta, was the hardest.

"I had to practice sticking my tongue through my teeth to get it right."

Frank started to understand how to run from class to class, although he thought it was a stupid system, convinced it would be better if the teachers moved around. The dumbest parts of school were gym classes. Baseball was the most boring. He was used to soccer where there is movement all the time. He stood still waiting for the ball to come to him, wearing an oversized glove. He thought, *Can't these Americans catch a little ball without a glove?"*

Then there was football, which seemed totally absurd. Frank could not catch or throw the ball because it wasn't round.

"I watched as someone caught the ball and ran. Everyone else sprinted after that boy. When the runners caught up with the kid who had the ball, a bunch of players jumped on top of him. A whistle blew. Everybody got up and patted each other on the behind. I didn't get it," he said.

"Maybe that's why you watch CNN instead of football," I said.

"The strangest part of gym was track," he said. "We were forced to go outside wearing shorts in cold weather—shorts—and it was much colder than in Bat Yam. First we ran to a black area that surrounded the football field. I didn't understand why we had to jog around the track. We ran and ran around and around, chasing each other in a big circle. I was sweaty and exhausted. Then we took a shower in the middle of the day. I would have preferred a good run with my dog, Kushy."

Frank's first report card gave him good marks in daily work habits: listening, class citizenship, trying hard. His teacher wrote: "*It is a pleasure to work with Frank as he is alert, cooperative and friendly. He is doing his best, but he does not understand the language well enough to do satisfactory work. His effort is good.*"

17: Keeping in Touch

*1947   July 26: President Harry S. Truman presents The
Truman Doctrine to a joint session of Congress
officially declaring the start of The Cold War against
communism.*

*November 29:   UN Special Committee on Palestine
recommends the partition of Palestine into two
states: one Arab, one Jewish.*

*The textile industry in the USA leads the world in
automatic looms, often replacing workers.*

*Development of synthetic fibers threatens the cotton
industry.*

Frank kept up a correspondence with Chezzi and his old
classmates in Bat Yam. He sent a dollar—when he could—
to the Jewish National Fund that was dedicated to create a
Jewish state or to plant trees. His former classmates wrote
back, a message dictated to his friend Yaron because Yaron
had the best handwriting in the group.

We are sure that you left us for a short period of time to put your eyes in the big wide world. . . .From the first day we felt that somebody was missing within our class and it became clear it was you. We looked around in the morning exercise and you were not there. With the dollar we received from you we will plant a tree. We understand from your words that you will be back.

We have a few questions to ask you. Are there Jewish schools in your new land? What are your studies like regarding history and geography and math? Is it very different from ours? Do you feel different? Are you already fluent in English? Is it your day-to-day language? Do you have problems in grammar? What language is spoken by most of the Jews, Hebrew or Yiddish? How is the weather in New York? Are you already feeling spring? Are there any magazines in Hebrew?

Later in the year the politics of the Middle East heated up and the letters became more serious.

To Yaakov, our classmate in the Diaspora (outside the motherland) shalom (hello) with a blessing. The government has opened up against us. The new body of law is the military army. Tel Aviv is closed and surrounded. Nobody goes out or comes in. The city stands like a dot, alone, surrounded with barbed wire. All services of the post office and telephone have been closed. The supply of food has become difficult. Some people are separated from their homes because of the very sudden military operation. Many of the teachers of our school cannot come to us and the students who are studying in schools in Tel Aviv have arranged for a limited period of time to study in our classes. With all of this, the way of studies goes on in the usual rhythm.

Your monthly contribution you sent us never arrived. The letter was opened and the dollar had been taken out. Your grandmother agreed she would pay the dollar to buy a tree.

Frank also wrote letters to his *opi* until May of 1947 when he and *omi* Marta came to live with them in the States.

"My grandparents gave my dog to cousin Gidi Elden," Frank said. "That's when I realized I would never see Kushy again."

Opi and *omi* believed that material possessions were not as important as life, freedom and family. They left their furniture and washing machine for their friend Kurt Eishal and closed the door, much as their daughter Hilda and Fred had done when they left Berlin.

"But Kushy was my friend," Frank said. "Not a material possession and I felt empty even though I knew the dog was going to be well cared for."

Frank started to look for other ways to connect. He joined the Boy Scouts, Troop Five, in Larchmont. He made some good friends there and went camping with them in the summer. He was selected to be in The Order of the Arrow, Scouting's National Honor Society.

"I was getting used to my new life," Frank said.

In Larchmont Frank's parents kept the bedroom. Ada slept in the dinette and Frank shared the living room with his grandparents. Even though his mother was glad they were all together, there was no privacy.

"I didn't mind because I had my *opi* again. Within six months we moved again. My parents had found a house."

Hilda and Fred thought Larchmont was way too fancy, too materialistic and too expensive. They preferred the East Bronx where they bought a small brick house on an unpaved road with a driveway that slanted downward. The house had a single-car garage and a garden in the back where Frank's father could plant an apple tree. They were walking distance from Evander Childs High School and near the subway for his dad. Before they moved, *opi* Martin suffered a heart attack and died. He was 75.

"I was told he passed away quietly at work in a new rubber recycling factory he was building for someone in Brooklyn," Frank said. "My parents wouldn't allow me to attend the funeral."

"Weren't you angry?" I asked.

"Maybe," he said, always reluctant to have a negative thought. "I was very sad, especially during the seven days of *Shiva*, the period of mourning, but my parents were trying to protect me from further sadness."

Years later Frank learned that his *opi* had collapsed climbing subway stairs, surrounded by strangers, causing a commotion, unable to be saved. His death had not been as peaceful as Frank had been told.

"I realized for the first time that my mother and father probably kept many things from me. They wanted me to experience a happy childhood in the midst of evil and chaos."

"Why did you listen to your parents?" I asked. "Why didn't you insist on going to the funeral?"

"That's what we did back then," Frank said. "When our parents told us what to do, we listened."

Frank certainly didn't want to move to the Bronx. He didn't want to face another new beginning and new school just as he was starting to belong somewhere. He continued to write letters to Chezzi, and now he wanted to keep in contact with his new friends.

"My parents agreed to drive me to scout meetings in Larchmont," Frank said, "so I could stay in touch. But after awhile, those relationships faded."

18: The Bronx

1948 Gentleman's Agreement, *about anti-Semitism in the United States, wins Academy Award for best motion picture.*

May 14: Israel becomes an independent state.

1949 North Atlantic Treaty Organization (NATO) is formed.

"For the first time I had my own room with my own closet that was built into the wall," Frank said. "I was 14, living in the Bronx and I remember thinking, *maybe things aren't so bad after all, but I'm still going back to Bat Yam when I graduate.*

Evander Childs High School was bigger than his school in Mamaroneck. There were 4,000 kids—1,000 in Frank's graduating class. The school took up one square city block and was four stories high.

"Best of all we had a pool so I joined the swim team specializing in the breaststroke. My father came to all the meets," Frank said. "I was very skinny and one time when I jumped into the pool for a medley in a New York City championship competition, my bathing suit slipped off. I didn't know what to do so I just kept swimming."

Frank's speed helped his team win and earned him a favored place among his teammates. His popularity further increased when his high school won the city championship seven times.

"It was a tribute to our coach, Bill Gay," Frank said.

"Now that I was settled, I tried to think of ways I could earn money. I remembered delivering my dad's used newspaper to neighbors in Bat Yam and wondered how the teachers at school each received a newspaper on their desk in the morning. At Evander Childs I found a job delivering papers to all the seniors who were studying current events. I arrived at school at 7:00 a.m., picked up three big bundles of *The Herald Tribune,* then separated and delivered 150 papers to the students."

Frank was still having trouble with English. To fulfill his high school language requirement he took classes in both German and Hebrew.

"The lessons were backwards for me," he said, "but studying languages in which I was fluent helped pull up my average while I learned English. I even became president of the Hebrew Club. I didn't realize it then, but I was starting to feel at home in America."

On weekends the family often drove to Larchmont to visit the rest of their relatives.

"It was hard because Grandma Alice would give ice cream to my cousins, but not to Ada or me, even though we were standing right there," Frank said. "We really wanted some ice cream but were afraid to ask. I still don't know why we were left out."

His cousins saw it differently. They lived with their grandma and have fonder memories.

"On the other hand," Frank said, "sometimes Alice was very generous. When I finally celebrated my bar mitzvah on my 14th birthday, she bought me a soccer ball and a beautiful used blue bicycle. I made snow chains for it so I could ride to school in the snow. Back in Bat Yam I had dreamed about these two gifts. I was happy to have them, but I also felt terrible because I couldn't share my soccer ball with my team at my old school and I couldn't ride my bike with my real friends back home."

Frank's classmates wrote often, especially Chezzi who told about the conflict with the British, the violence, the demonstrations—the serious sides of life. He discussed the United Nations vote for a new country called Israel and the celebrations all over the land with free taxi rides and free ice cream when independence became official in 1948.

Chezzi told Frank, "We have a big responsibility on our shoulders. Remember, the nation has not been built yet and one needs to give it some shape, like a baby that has just been born."

"How I longed to be part of that movement," Frank said. "I could hardly wait to go back. Chezzi and I were children in the Middle East. Our knowledge of human predicaments and choices were on a more sophisticated level than my American friends. In the States kids talked about baseball and football, homework and popular music––things that had nothing to do with the love of the land."

Nat King Cole and Frank Sinatra were on the radio. Peggy Lee sang *Mañana* and Kay Kyser sang about Woody the Woodpecker.

"I didn't know or care about what a woodpecker was and I didn't understand the silly laugh that was part of the song. I was unhappy to be so removed from events surrounding the founding of the state of Israel. Of course there were many important political situations going on in America, but I didn't know about them. They were not yet part of my blood."

At school history and civics were the most challenging classes. Frank had to learn about a government with an executive branch, a Senate and a House of Representatives, as well as local mayors, governors, cities, counties, states and a nation. There was history with Pilgrims wearing funny hats and Indians sharing corn and a gold rush and a Civil War and international relations.

"It was too much to put in order, especially in English," Frank said. "My new friend, Marty Silver, helped me. If I didn't understand a question on a test, I would whisper, 'eight,' and he would say 'A' or 'B' or whatever the answer was."

Marty couldn't swim. In exchange for his help on tests, when the gym teacher called Marty's name to take his swim test, Frank jumped into the water and swam for him. The school was so big the teachers didn't know the difference and Marty passed.

"I did the same for Frank Agardy, my new best friend who also couldn't swim though he was president of the class," Frank said. "Agardy's parents were immigrants from Hungary. Despite the fact that he was Christian, we understood each other. On Christmas Mrs. Agardy always had a present for me under their tree."

One day Marty and Frank went to the marshes where Co-Op City now stands. They fished for crabs and had a great time. Unfortunately, Marty lost a big gold ring in the cold water. It had belonged to his father who had recently died.

"Marty was devastated," Frank said. "That night I got up at 4:00 a.m. and rode my bike back to the marshes. Having lived near the sea, I knew it would be low tide. I found Marty's ring lodged between the rocks and was back home before I had to get up for school. My parents never knew I had left."

Frank's next big excitement was getting his junior driver's license. By then he had started dating and his father would drive him—and his date—to Westchester where a junior license was legal. While Fred visited Uncle Herbert, Frank would take the car and drive his date to a movie, then pick his father up for the ride back. Sometimes Frank and his dad went for a drive by themselves. They talked about Frank returning to Israel after graduation.

"My father told me that if I went back so soon, I would earn a living using my muscles—farming or herding goats and sheep. But if I went to college in America, I could return a little later with some expertise and skills that would be more important to Israel. I began to think a lot about what he said."

While he considered his future, Frank's dad took him on his first ski trip. In Germany Fred had been a great skier. He even asked his in-laws to ship his skis and boots from Germany to Palestine and then to America. Father and son took a bus to Hunter Mountain in Upstate New York and skiing became one of the passions Frank later passed along to his sons.

When Frank was old enough to have a senior driver's license, he drove his friends Herbie and Barry on dates with stops at White Castle for burgers. That summer, between his junior and senior years in high school, Frank worked at a hotel in the Catskills.

"I picked up visitors from the train or bus stations and drove them to the resort," he said. "Sometimes I helped in the dining room. The women I waited on would not order from the menu. They said, 'Bring it on, boy. Bring it all on.' They ate everything. They were fatter than any group I had ever seen."

It was fun, but Frank's dad wanted him to have other experiences so that he could figure out a career.

"I came home to work in a printing plant, a machine shop, an iron repair store and a shop that sold commercial refrigeration systems in the Bronx," he said. "My father had lots of connections and every few weeks he helped me find something new to try."

The next summer Frank's father sent him to work in a textile factory at the Bruck Silk Mills, Herbert's good client in Cowansville, Quebec. Everyone spoke French so once again Frank relied upon body language and facial expressions to communicate. He started out in a local hotel but soon befriended another worker who invited him to board with his family at half the cost. Frank blended in with Mr. and Mrs. Liberty and their ten other children and he earned enough to pay for the trip as well as his room and meals.

"I worked in a spinning room that was at least as big as a football field. It was filled with machines that spun fiber into yarn. There were so many machines it sounded like an airplane taking off, so we wore earplugs. Workers removed the spun yarn from the machines and put them into carts to be wheeled to a weaving room with over 100 looms. I couldn't believe it was even noisier than the spinning room. The sound was so loud I couldn't hear anyone talk. I was glad to be transferred to the dye house," Frank said.

In the early part of his senior year, everyone was gearing up for college. Frank's parents did not understand the American educational system. They couldn't help him, so the school gave Frank a number of aptitude tests. Results indicated he should become a forest ranger, a policeman or an automobile mechanic.

"I wonder how they made this decision," Frank said. "I had never seen a forest and didn't know what a forest ranger was."

Still planning to return to Israel, Frank decided to study agricultural engineering. After his father drove him to see some schools, he was accepted at the University of Connecticut. Finally Frank faced a new beginning he was looking forward to. This time he would keep his name and identity.

Evander Childs' graduation was impressive. The 1,000 kids in his class, together with their parents and siblings, filled the Paramount Theater on the Grand Concourse.

"I felt very important wearing my cap and gown," he said. "If I'd stayed in Bat Yam, I would have gone to high school in Tel Aviv, if at all."

After living in America for five years, Frank's parents applied to become naturalized citizens. His sister would be included automatically because she was only 13. Since Frank was 18 he was required to go through the process on his own. But he decided to wait. He wasn't sure he would become an American although he now stood for the pledge of allegiance to the flag and enjoyed singing *The Star Spangled Banner* with his friends. Still, he was not ready to let go of his Middle Eastern identity.

How could he know that it would take only 18 months living away at college for him to change his mind? He had no idea he would soon conquer his civic history lessons and join the rest of his family as a naturalized American citizen. He couldn't anticipate that many years later he would help reclaim land—not in Israel but in America.

"After my high school graduation ceremony, my family and I went to Krum's ice cream parlor on the Grand Concourse between 188th Street and Fordham Road across from the Loew's Paradise Theater," Frank said.

"My parents were both born in America," I said. "My mother grew up on Morris Avenue in the Bronx and my dad on Clay Avenue. My mom used to love Sutter's bakery, also on the Grand Concourse and Fordham Road. Years later, for special occasions we would drive from our home in Westchester to get cakes with apricot filling and mocha frosting. What did you order to celebrate your graduation?" I asked Frank.

"Ah," Frank smiled, lost in memories. "If Krum's still existed, I would go there for a chocolate egg cream and maybe even stop at White Castle for a burger, but for my graduation I ordered Coca Cola, my favorite drink."

19: Three Colleges To Get It Right

*1952   Israel and Germany agree to retribution of damages
to Jews by Nazis.*

1953   Frank becomes a naturalized American citizen.

"They assigned a pig to me," Frank said about his first days
at college. "It was a sow, an animal I had never seen in Bat
Yam."

After high school Frank's friends, Marty Silver and
Frank Agardy, commuted to City College. The school had a
great reputation and it would have been comfortable for
him to join them, as if it were an extension of high school.
If he followed their path, Frank would continue to live
home, speak German in the house, take the subway to class,
schedule car time with his father for dates and visit
relatives on Sundays.

"It was familiar, but I wanted a new experience.
Besides, farming was not offered at City College and I was
determined to learn skills to work the land."

Frank convinced his parents to visit a few schools
on the East Coast then chose the University of Connecticut
because they let him major in Agricultural Engineering. Of

course he was required to join the 4-H Club, a youth organization embracing thinking, caring, working and living well (head, heart, hands and health). His assignment was to enter a pig in a contest at a country fair.

"My pig was enormous, maybe 600 pounds. I remember polishing the hoofs with black polish and using white buck shoe powder to buff out spots on its skin," he said. "Then I walked the pig in a circle. As the judges marked their papers I pretended to care if we won. I couldn't understand why the pig listened to me, why it didn't trample my feet or run away. The other kids seemed to think it was fun."

Many things about Frank and U-Conn were mismatched, but he couldn't figure out what was wrong.

"On day one I stuck out my hand to greet my roommate," Frank said. "The boy was older and had completed a stint in the military. *An All American,* I thought. *This will be great.* Instead of a smile and friendly hello, the guy drew an imaginary line down the center of the room. 'You stay on your side,' he said. 'I'll stay on mine.' *Maybe that's how it is in New England* I thought, losing some of the confidence I had when I lived in my old neighborhood. Maybe my accent annoyed him."

Teddy Rosenberg was assigned to the room across the hall. He was another freshman and came over to say hello.

"My roommate told him to stay away from his side of the room," Frank said.

Teddy was appalled. "What? Are you kidding?" he asked.

A fight broke out between them. A real fight using fists, punching. When it was over, Frank became Teddy's roommate. On the weekend they drove to Nyack in Teddy's Nash convertible.

"I met his dad who took us to his store, The Bee Hive, and told us we could have anything we needed to make our room our home," Frank said.

The semester was getting better, but it wasn't the experience Frank had hoped for. The other boys were rich. They had their own new cars and lots of spending money. Frank was paying for his education from summer employment and part-time jobs. The other kids liked to drink and party late into the night. Frank's parents drank wine on Friday nights for Shabbat so Frank had learned to drink only on special occasions.

"I became the designated driver," he said, "though nobody called it that at the time."

Frank was friendly and preferred not to stay by himself. When he was invited, he joined other kids, went along on activities even if they seemed silly or a little improper.

"Sometimes the boys walked right into the girls' dorms. Their walls were plastered with photos of a singer, a real famous guy. What's his name?" Frank said. "He married Debbie Reynolds and then that dark-haired beauty."

"Do you mean Eddie Fisher?" I asked.

"Yes. That's the one," he said. "I still don't get why everybody was so excited about him or why anyone paid attention when he switched wives. I didn't relate to these kids and I hated studying the required chemistry and physics courses. Maybe I should have gone to City College. Studying farming wasn't what I had hoped it would be."

During his summer vacation Frank worked for a commercial refrigeration company that sold and repaired refrigeration machinery in bars, restaurants and food stores not far from his home.

"It was a small company run by an elderly Jewish man who took his son and me to different sections of the

New York City," Frank said. "Every morning I got up early, walked to Pelham Parkway to catch a bus to the Grand Concourse then took another bus to meet him on149[th] Street to drive to Manhattan. We walked the avenues making cold calls to see if shop owners needed to improve their refrigeration systems. I took one side of the block and his son took the other. We'd meet at the corner to compare notes then tackle the next block. I wasn't shy and I loved working with machines. It was a hot summer and I always found someone who needed help to cool his environment. I realized I was very good at understanding anything with a motor."

On one excursion the owner of a bar grabbed Frank. "I need your help," he said. "My ice cubes are coming out red. Could be blood."

Frank was too scared to say no. He followed the man to the back then opened the freezer.

"I almost threw up," he said. "There were parts of an animal, all gray and hairy. I could see it was a cat, a bony cat. I was afraid to ask if it was somebody's pet or how it got there. Sections of its tail had been cut into squares. I called my buddy and we removed all the parts then stuffed them into a bag. It was disgusting. We cleaned out the whole machine with our bare hands, no gloves."

In appreciation the owner served them a private lunch—a huge seafood meal, Frank's first taste of lobster and crabmeat.

"It was so good," Frank said, "we went back one night but cops were sitting in a car outside surveying the area. They wouldn't let us in. Evidently the bar was where locals placed illegal bets. I never found out who the police were looking for."

A week later Frank was back at U-Conn, hating his studies and socializing with kids who were on more academic or business tracks instead of the kids in his agricultural classes. He decided to transfer to another school.

"As long as I was transferring, I might as well change my major. I thought it would be a simple switch. Instead of studying agriculture I would study engineering. But if I gave up farming, would I still return to the Middle East? For the first time I considered the possibility of not going back right after graduation. I didn't realize that changing my major was the beginning of a permanent life in America."

Frank applied to Long Island Agricultural and Technical Institute in Farmingdale, New York, a two-year community college. He gravitated to the technical side of the school.

"I wanted to major in Refrigeration, Heating and Air Conditioning as part of an applied science degree—a practical engineering degree."

Farmingdale was on a trimester system and U-Conn was organized on a two-semester system. Everyone told Frank he'd have to lose the rest of the year, but he was in a hurry to finish his education and get on with his life.

"Waiting made no sense to me so I put on one of those old ties you threw out—the skinny wool ones—and went to the school to convince someone to let me in immediately."

"You had over 50 out-of-style ties you never wore," I said. "When we merged our homes, you said you didn't need to keep them."

"I wanted to make you happy," he said. "But now I can't show you what I'm talking about."

"I remember," I said, trying not to roll my eyes. "And we still have your burgundy polyester patterned bell-bottom stretch pants. But why did you wear a tie to Farmingdale?" I asked refocusing our discussion.

"I wanted to impress the Dean," he said. "I went to his office and sat myself on his desk. I looked at him and said, 'I want to be in your school. I can't lose a semester. I can't wait. What's the difference to you when I start?' The Dean told me he never had a kid do that before, so he accepted me right there."

"I like your style," I said. "I did something similar when I was a fourth-grade school teacher with a New York State principal's license and wanted to change to the corporate world. Everyone said it was impossible. I put on a suit and new silk blouse, the uniform of the game I was entering, then took the Metro North train from Larchmont to Manhattan and selected buildings that were walking distance from Grand Central Station. In the elevators I pushed buttons at random and told the receptionists I was a teacher who was trainable and educable. In one company, an executive woman came out while I was standing there. 'I used to be a teacher,' she said. 'Can you write?'

"Yes," I said, though I wasn't sure. I landed my first communications assignment—interviewing teachers for an article about education. Before I left the office, I asked the woman, "Where am I?" so I could return with my article. You can call it luck, coincidence, moxie. I think it was meant to be and so was your journey into engineering."

"If you say so," Frank said, too pragmatic to waste time on a theoretical discussion, especially about past events.

By 1952 Frank was getting ready to graduate. The United States was in the midst of the Cold War with the Soviet Union that had acquired nuclear weapons. The Korean War was still raging, the Communist Revolution in China divided the mainland from Taiwan and Joseph McCarthy was hunting for communists in America.

"My friends asked me what I thought about the turmoil in the world and how it affected our nation and maybe even us," Frank said. "They wanted to know if I was going to vote for Eisenhower or Stevenson for President. I was too embarrassed to tell anyone I didn't know the difference between a Republican and a Democrat. I never paid attention because I couldn't vote. I wasn't an American citizen. It bothered me that my parents and my sister were citizens, a family united in America while I was a young man without a country. I began to follow political debates in the newspaper and decided to apply for citizenship."

Frank signed up for a naturalization course in Manhattan. It reminded him of his social studies classes in high school, only this time it was easier because he remembered so much.

"There were about 50 people and I guess most were older than I was. I sat next to someone from China on one side and someone from Mexico on the other. The older people seemed more nervous than the few who were closer to my age. I heard many different languages. For the first time I felt that being an immigrant was not so unusual. I wondered if the other people spoke a different tongue at home like we did. Did they cling to Spanish or Japanese or Chinese or Czech?"

After he was sworn in, Frank rode the subway to his father's office to meet his parents for a special lunch. This time they skipped the Horn & Hardart and celebrated in a restaurant at the top of the Pan Am Building.

"I remember sitting in my blue shirt and striped tie and looking out the oversized windows on to the New York skyline. I thought, 'this is my country now. This is really my city.'"

During Frank's graduation ceremony at Farmingdale the Dean gave a speech.

"I was shocked when he mentioned my interview with him. The Dean told the whole audience that I had earned straight A's," Frank said. "I felt proud to be singled out for an accomplishment rather than for being a man with an accent."

Graduation marked the completion of one phase of Frank's life. But it wasn't enough. Hilda and Fred had always emphasized the importance of a college degree, especially since they both had lost their opportunities to attend a university. By now Frank was familiar with the educational system in America. He knew he wanted more than a diploma from a community college.

"I had a friend who felt the same way," Frank said. "We searched the library for a school that would accept our credits and allow us to earn a four-year college degree in engineering. California State Polytechnic Institute in San Luis Obispo, California, sounded good in their catalog. But I wasn't sure. I had made a mistake before and I had never been that far away from my family. But my parents encouraged me to go. They didn't mind the distance as long as I could get a better education, as good as they imagined I might have gotten in Germany."

Hilda arranged for a friend of a friend who was going to settle in Alaska to take Frank to California.

"The man was a doctor so we all thought he must be smart, but he kept getting lost," Frank said. "I could read a map and became navigator as well as part-time driver."

The doctor's Ford Falcon reeked of cigar smoke and Chinese food he bought to fill his very fat body.

"On the positive side, I experienced the vastness of my new country, stopping in Chicago, Nebraska and Salt Lake City."

As they drove toward San Luis Obispo the weather and the vegetation began to change. The area smelled of flowers with the hint of a warm breeze from the nearby Pacific Ocean.

"It was like the Middle East," Frank said. "Even the buildings were simple square edifices. Their Spanish style smooth walls reminded me of my cement house in Bat Yam."

Classes were scientific so Frank's poor English didn't cause too many problems. He joined the swim team and competed on a state level. He took courses in the summer to catch up on time lost transferring twice and he logged in 60 hours flying solo in the flying club. It wasn't until his senior year that he realized how many directions he could take after graduation.

"Up until this moment I had followed my parents' lead. Then I followed required educational programs. I was impatient to take charge of my life. I wanted to create roots with one job, one place to live and one wife to share it all.

"I knew I would never live with my parents again," Frank said. "Beyond that, the choices were overwhelming."

20: Too Many Options

1950-1953 The Korean War.

1955 In opposition to the Western NATO Treaty, the Warsaw Pact aligns eight communist states in the Eastern Bloc including Czechoslovakia.

1959 IBM introduces computers to the business world.

"Out. I wanted out of college and into the job market. It was the only way I could be independent," Frank said.

In the middle of his senior year companies from across the country came to Cal Poly to mine for talent. Frank signed up to be interviewed by a few potential employers but his first choice was an aircraft company that was rumored to pay the highest wages.

"They questioned me for an hour," he said. "What did I study, what did I think of the Korean War, was I a United States citizen?"

They offered him a job for $600 a month. He was thrilled, but he wasn't sure he belonged in Texas, another new place far from his family.

"Then something beyond my control intervened," Frank said. "A kid in my dorm was impressed that I could speak German and Hebrew. I don't recall his name but I remember sitting together in the evening while he asked me questions about my life and my experience with machines. I thought he was fascinated with me because I had lived inside history surrounding WWII but it turns out he was sleuthing for his dad, a senior executive at Rohr Industries. At the time Rohr was the leading manufacturer of aircraft engine housing and parts. Their business was escalating and they were hiring engineers."

The kid's father offered Frank a job at $700 a month, more than any of his friends from the Cal Poly engineering department were earning.

"It was unimaginable to me to earn so much money and be able to stay in California," Frank said.

With one of his three goals checked off his list, Frank was ready for the next big event in his life, finding his future wife. Another friend, Ben Friedman, at Cal Poly invited him to a party arranged by girls Ben knew from Lake Arrowhead in the mountains not far from Los Angeles. The girls were students at UCLA.

"Just before the party, I developed pterygium in one eye, a benign growth that can interfere with vision. The problem supposedly comes from too much exposure to sun, low humidity and sand. Maybe it was something left over from my days in Bat Yam. Doctors told me to have an operation quickly, but I really wanted to go to the party."

Frank called Margit, the girl who was to host the event and managed to spend the day with her at her house in Beverly Hills. They quickly discovered they both had been born in Berlin and both their parents spoke German. After his operation Frank and Margit started dating.

Her parents, Max and Helga Ponder, made him feel like he belonged to her family. He got along well with her kid brother, also named Frank and her little sister, Renee. The family owned a small sheep dog named Schnapps who was friendlier than Kushy. Most important, Margit was terrific.

"Right away I knew I was home," Frank said. "If only I could commit."

The roads connecting San Luis Obispo and Los Angeles were not like today's highways. Despite the distance and inconvenience, Frank and Margit soon became an exclusive couple.

"I didn't mind long drives because seconds after I accepted the job," Frank said, "I borrowed $500 from my dad to purchase a used Oldsmobile."

Meanwhile, Rohr Industries conducted a background check on all potential new hires, including Frank. They sent representatives to Mickle Avenue in the Bronx to interview his parents and neighbors. They spoke to his friends in New York and at Cal Poly and to his sister, Ada, who had flown to California for his upcoming graduation.

"I took part in my commencement on a Sunday and started work on Monday," Frank said.

His clearance was at such a high level he was given a special nametag indicating he was vital to the industry. He could work in all sections of the plant.

Rohr Industries was located in Chula Vista, south of San Diego, yet close enough for Frank to drive to see Margit at UCLA. After she graduated she accepted a fourth-grade teaching position near the Rohr plant.

"I also taught fourth grade," I said to Frank. "That's an odd coincidence."

"Not really," he said. "Many women were teachers in those days. My mother gave me a special ring for Margit, but I couldn't move forward. I kept it in my pocket for over two months trying to decide whether she was right for me."

You did the same thing with me, I thought.

One evening at dinner with the Ponders, Renee piped up in her 7-year-old voice, "When are you going to pop the question, Frank?"

The whole family stopped talking. There was silence except for the sound of everyone breathing.

"I believed Margit and I were right for each other," Frank said, "but what if I were wrong? What if she wasn't as wonderful as I assumed?"

His dad told him to take a piece of paper and write down the pros and cons of the relationship. Once he made his decision, he tore up the lists. Frank stopped calculating and found the courage to become engaged, confident Margit was to be his one true love. They married on June 21, 1959.

"Though the party was in a tent in the Ponders' backyard, it was fancier than any wedding I'd been to," Frank said. "My list of guests was small. It included my parents, grandmother, sister, Uncle Herbert and Aunt Stella and cousins Laurel, Beryl and Jeff, as well as a few friends from New York and Cal Poly."

There were endless discussions about ushers. He chose Margit's brother, Frank Ponder, Margit's cousin, Frank Stagen and Frank Agardy, his friend from the Bronx. They were labeled The Four Franks. The bulk of the 150 people were Margit's family and friends and many of her dad's business associates.

"Margit looked gorgeous in her long white gown with lace sleeves," Frank said. "I wore a light blue dinner jacket with a black satin bow tie and my Roy Orbison glasses. They were very fashionable at the time."

On weekends they drove to her parents' house on Lake Arrowhead where the air was clearer and cooler than in Los Angeles. He loved the smell of pine trees from the surrounding forest where he walked with Margit's dad, Max.

"At the lake I learned to water ski. I started by jumping off the pier on one ski," he said. "I didn't want to stop for the winter so I put Max's 20 ft. Flattie sailboat on a trailer and hauled it to the San Diego Harbor. I jumped on and figured out how to sail around the large Navy ships. When the winds shifted, I had to make sure the boom didn't hit me on the head."

"How could you do this without lessons?" I asked.

"By feel. I felt the wind and figured the proper angles."

His actions were a bit more scientific at Rohr Industries. The company was huge, with more employees than the population of Bat Yam. As a plant engineer, Frank was given a golf cart to circulate from department to department to solve any engineering problems related to air conditioning and heating systems.

"You must have been important," I said.

"I knew what I was doing. I worked with titanium honeycombs—metal structures that are strong enough to sustain high wind pressure and move an airplane wing up or down when flying. My assignment was to create wing sections for B-58 airplanes by tapering the honeycombs from eight-inch sections into quarter inch sections by using a milling machine."

"Did you wear goggles?" I asked.

Frank smiled. "No. I didn't DO it," he said with a shrug. "I developed the technology using nitrogen to strengthen the honeycomb before milling."

Fred Rohr noticed Frank's abilities and asked him to build a dining room table with two Lazy Susans for his new house. The table was to have electric controls to enable Rohr to raise the tables by pushing a button. Another button would work the curtains and still another, the lights. A fourth button would move the dining room table into the floor to create a space to dance.

"I helped create an environment I had never imagined existed anywhere," Frank said, "not even in someone's head."

Then everything changed. The Korean War began to ebb. There were fewer demands for aircraft engine parts. Rohr invested in IBM 650 computers to handle paychecks for thousands of employees.

Frank supervised the installation of the computers on the roof. He placed them in a special air-conditioned structure designed to lower the tremendous heat the computers emitted. The reduced demand for engineers and the ability of computers to replace bookkeepers led to major layoffs.

"I was 27 years old," Frank said. "I was a star yet I was filled with dread. When would I be fired? Though I had wanted my job to last forever, I decided not to wait until I became obsolete."

Margit and Frank used this as an opportunity to try something else, to explore Europe before they started a family. Her dad had a contact in London who placed Frank with G. N. Haden & Sons, an engineering consultant firm.

"My assignment was to design air conditioning systems for Barclay's Bank in Ghana," Frank said. "Since I could do this from my drafting table in London, it was a perfect chance to live and work in England and to see the surrounding regions."

They rented two rooms in Hampstead Gardens, a suburb in North West London. On weekends they traveled to the White Cliffs of Dover, the canals in Amsterdam and the Eiffel Tower in Paris, all on a tight budget. The best was Zürs in Austria where they both improved their ability to ski, flying down slopes, whizzing through the early part of their marriage, exploring every nearby area.

"It was a fantastic time in our lives," Frank said, "but wherever we walked, especially in London, we saw buildings with bullet holes and bombed-out sections from the war. They reminded me of stories my mother and father had told and I realized how lucky I was that my family had left Berlin. I wanted to visit Germany to see my history and what had become of my parents' past."

21: Mucki Returns

1961 Upon Soviet instruction, The German Democratic Republic built a concrete wall topped with barbed wire to stop emigration from East to West.

The film, Judgment at Nuremberg, *is released.*

Margit's dad, Max, was in Germany to meet with the Rolleiflex camera company as their sales rep for the Western United States.

"Max rarely talked about his early life," Frank said, "so when he invited us to be his guests at the Kempinski Hotel in Berlin we welcomed the opportunity to see where Margit's family had come from as well as to enjoy the luxury of a five-star hotel. Of course I also had my own history to explore."

It was 1961 and Berlin was in the midst of the communist side of Germany. Their visit was just before the Berlin Wall went up so it was still possible for Westerners to travel in and out of the city without much difficulty.

If they drove to Berlin, they would be stopped at the East German border and given a ticket stamped with the time of entry. Their ticket would be stamped again upon their arrival in Berlin. If too much time elapsed while they were in Communist territory, if they visited relatives along the way, they would have to pay a substantial fine or be delayed for questioning about their activities. They opted to fly in from London.

"We read that bombs had flattened the city, but the button factory once owned by Max's father-in-law stood without any major destruction," Frank said. "It was part of a group of buildings with a central garage area. The family driver still lived in the gatehouse. He was amazed to see Max, glad to learn he had survived."

Max told the old driver that he had left Berlin with his wife, Helga, and baby, Margit, to catch one of the last ships from Hamburg to London in 1939. From London they had boarded another ship to New York then traveled to San Francisco and finally settled in Los Angeles. Helga's sister arrived a few months later.

"We had heard this story before," Frank said. "But Margit was hungry for more details so Max took us to the apartment building where Margit was born. It, too, had not been damaged. Downstairs was a dress shop where she bought a print dress for my sister's upcoming wedding in New York."

Max left and Frank and Margit took a taxi to Frank's first neighborhood. Since they spoke German and Frank's folks had shared so many stories he felt familiar with the street and the house.

"But those were my parents' memories," Frank said. "I needed to create my own."

Frank rang one of the three doorbells on the right side of the front metal gate. Nobody answered. He tried again; reluctant to leave #10 Wilheimstrasse in what was then the French section of Berlin where he had been born 28 years earlier. He was disappointed he would not meet

Mrs. Velzine, the woman who had cared for him as an infant, the one who had nicknamed him Mucki.

"I always wondered who she was, what she was like," Frank said. "I stood mesmerized looking at her name and remembering her little dachshund that had inspired me to buy my wooden black dog on my way from Venice to Palestine in 1936."

The stone house was in great condition with a fresh coat of white paint trimmed in dark blue. The verandas on each side of the building had red awnings and pots of red geraniums. There were more red geraniums in the windows.

"Now that I was in front of my house I couldn't believe I wouldn't be able to get inside," he said. "I refused to accept that Mrs. Velzine wasn't home. My feet seemed separated from my body, glued to the sidewalk. I couldn't get myself to leave."

He looked around and noticed a small grocery store on the ground level of a private house across the street.

"I had not been told any stories about this store," Frank said. "But something pulled me in."

Sausages hung from the low ceiling. Frank inhaled the smell of good smoked fish and recognized hearty brown breads he ate at home. A gray-haired woman, perhaps in her late 60s was standing behind a thick, well-worn wooden counter. She had big hands and wore a green apron.

"Do you happen to know Mrs. Velzine?" Frank asked in German.

"Yes, I know her well," she said. "She's working and will be back tonight. But what business is it of yours?"

"I lived in that house across the street until I was almost 3 years old," Frank said. "We left in 1936 right after the Olympics."

The woman stiffened then grabbed the wooden counter with her heavy large hands, seeming to hold on with all her strength. Her face became red as she turned her head to the right and shouted, "Herman, you must come out. Mucki Levy is here!"

"Shocked, I shouted for Margit to come inside," Frank said.

A stout man with a cane limped out from behind an olive green curtain that probably separated their living quarters from the store. "Did your parents survive?" the woman asked. Before he could answer, they threw out more questions. "Where are they? How are they? We all knew what was going on. We couldn't do anything. We knew everything. Yes, we knew everything. We knew what happened to the Jews. We couldn't do anything to stop it without getting transported."

Frank didn't get a chance to respond. She kept talking.

"They left suddenly, your parents, but first they had an open house to sell their belongings. All the neighbors went to the sale. I remember their bedroom set—custom made out of gnarled lemon wood."

They talked about the war and how it was difficult for them. Her husband was wounded in the army, the Nazi army. They said they often talked about the Levy family, wondering if they had survived.

More than 25 years had passed since Frank's parents had left their home city.

"My mother and father never mentioned this woman or her store or life in those days," Frank said. "Perhaps their minds were already in Palestine. Mother always said, 'To leave one's country is not a luxury.' My parents always looked forward, not back."

Frank couldn't help wondering what these simple German citizens knew about the extermination of millions of people. Why they and all the other German citizens couldn't do anything to stop the Nazis, especially in the earlier years. No matter what the couple said, he kept wondering whether or not they had been members of the

Nazi party or silent citizens, themselves victims of this horrific maelstrom.

"I thought of one of our neighbors in Larchmont," Frank said. "He was born in that area. He attended school there. He married a local girl, raised his children in the same town and never traveled. For all I know, his major thoughts are what movie to see, where to buy his next car and where his children will go to college."

"Just like me," I said, beginning to understand what Frank was saying.

"I was sad for my parents," Frank said, "and critical of the one-dimensional years our neighbor experienced. Perhaps I am being unfair, a bit jealous of his consistent life."

Before Margit and Frank continued their journey, the lady behind the counter told him, "We had a son soon after you left. We named him Mucki."

22: Going Back

1962   Cuban Missile Crisis between the Soviet Union and Cuba versus the USA.

1963   November 22:   John F. Kennedy is assassinated.

1964   Students demonstrate against the Vietnam War.

The first jolt was when they left the ship in Haifa. The Israeli government seized their car, demanding $3,000 to get it out of customs. The duty was imposed to deter them from selling it on the black market for double its value. They were promised their money back when they left the country with the car.

"With all my talk about returning to Bat Yam to work the land, in 16 years I had never gone back, not even for a few days," Frank said. "Life had gotten in the way. I didn't want to fly in for a short visit like a tourist. I wanted to stay for a while. How else could I reconnect? I mean really reconnect and maybe even recover experiences I had missed? Margit had never been to Israel. In 1962 I arranged for us to stay for eight weeks, enough time to show her my memories. Now we had no car. What an uncomfortable beginning to a long overdue reunion."

When his contract with G.N. Haden had ended, Margit and Frank had driven their Hillman convertible from London to Naples where they boarded a ship to Haifa. They wanted to approach Israel from the sea, as most of the refugees had during and soon after the war. As they came near land they could see Mt. Carmel, a coastal mountain range in northern Israel. Margit was thrilled to be so close to history and to all the beauty. Frank had mixed feelings.

"Actually, I'm not sure how I felt," he said. "I had become an American and liked living in the States. Would I feel conflicted when I touched Israeli soil? Would this trip stir up old loyalties and influence me to reconsider my future? What opportunities would I have if we stayed? How was I going to get around without our car?"

They didn't have much cash so they left the automobile and took a taxi to visit Chezzi's sister, Miriam, who was expecting them. She and her husband, Kurt, owned a large chicken farm north of Tel Aviv and had plenty of room for visitors.

Years later their son, Yoram, would live with Frank for six months while he was working in New York City and looking for an apartment. Later Yoram married an American and settled on Long Island.

"We arrived in time to help fill an order for 2,000 live chickens that were to be trucked to a nearby kibbutz," Frank said. "Margit and I placed two chickens in each hand then carried them to wooden crates. We did this all afternoon."

"Margit carried live, clucking chickens?" I asked.

"Yes," Frank said. "We were a team. She lifted them by the wings."

I would never do that, I thought.

"In Israel I felt like my childhood never left me," Frank said. "The smell of falafel in a local restaurant carried secrets I had shared with my grandfather in the *souk*. A donkey tied to a tree near a shop made me rub my eyes remembering my operation. A child flying a kite followed the wind before I could show him how to make it go higher."

The next day Frank pushed to leave early to catch a bus to Jerusalem to be with Chezzi. They had not seen each other since 1946. They had morphed from boys into men, taller with young wives. Chezzi's eyes, as blue as the Mediterranean Sea, locked Frank's brown eyes that were now buffered behind glasses. Their smiles spoke more than paragraphs.

"I felt our old kinship boil up as we hugged," Frank said. "It was like we never parted. Chezzi had been a serious child with just enough wit to make me smile. Here I was, listening to details of his life and smiling again."

Chezzi was already the Director of the B'nai B'rith Women's Residential Treatment Center for emotionally disturbed children in Jerusalem.

"He escorted us through the home for boys, greeting every child by name," Frank said. "Each boy responded, 'Good morning, Chezzi.' It was so informal, so unlike a *yekke* to allow younger people to address him by his first name. Somehow it fit with Chezzi's philosophy of hugs not drugs."

By day three, Frank's dad called from America. He had arranged for his old friend, Mr. Metzger, to give Frank a promissory note that enabled him to get his car out of Haifa.

"Mr. Metzger worked with an Israeli financial group," Frank said, "so I guess his note had enough financial backing to satisfy the government. Now Margit and I had wheels to visit Bat Yam without worrying about bus schedules."

Miriam, Kurt and Chezzi wanted to come with them. Chezzi's wife, Talma, was a professional pianist who had studied in Paris. She had already scheduled piano lessons and was near the end of her first pregnancy so she stayed home. The other five friends piled into the Hillman and drove south through Jaffa. Since Margit didn't understand Hebrew, the friends spoke German as they had done with their parents.

"There were fewer Arab people than I remembered," Frank said. "We passed the clock tower. The black horse-drawn carriages that had been around the area were gone. We didn't stop until we reached the brewery at the beginning of the Bat Yam border. I took a deep breath, inhaling the sea and thought: *I am home. Or am I?*"

Chezzi's house had been about 100 yards further. It was still there, overlooking the sea. But Chezzi's mother had moved to Tel Aviv.

"Nobody welcomed us," Frank said. "Strangers lived in the house. There was no place for us to sit in the sand like we did as kids. The structures were the same, but my past was gone. The Bat Yam in my head no longer existed. I couldn't go back because going back meant picking up at the point my parents' had whisked me off to America. Impossible."

On the right was a road, the same road Frank's dad had used to drive their Willys down to the beach. But it wasn't the same. It was paved. They continued walking to the beach, stopping in front of the first rock called Adam.

"Some kids were chasing each other and laughing, but of course I didn't know them," Frank said. "I removed my shoes to feel the sand in my toes and realized I wasn't wearing sandals. How did I become a foreigner here, dressed in foreign clothes?"

They walked up the road to their old school. Kids were playing soccer in the schoolyard. They had a real ball.

"How did the school shrink? How did it get smaller than I remembered?" Frank said.

They turned down Balfour Street where Frank's house used to be. The Scharnitzky grocery store was still there but not Mr. Scharnitzky. Along the way they stopped in front of an old friend's house.

"Chezzi told me our friend had been killed in the war," Frank said. "I don't know which war."

At the end of Balfour Street we found a dirt road in the dunes. My concrete house was still there with the same concrete balcony. The owners let us in. It had not been painted or changed in sixteen years. There were cracks in the walls. An electric wire dangled from the ceiling in the living room where my parents' light fixture had hung. The bathrooms were just like I remembered, including the one that housed our boiler that had to be stoked with wood. In the kitchen the basic design of the marble counters were the same. Only the refrigerator had been replaced.

During their eight-week visit, Talma gave birth to a child that would be the first of their four children, a boy named Yuval, with his father's big blue eyes. Yuval would one day earn an MBA from Harvard, perhaps thanks to Frank, who encouraged him to apply.

A few days after Chezzi's son was born, Frank and Chezzi finally carved out extensive time to be together. Chezzi had a meeting in Haifa, a lengthy bus ride. Frank volunteered to drive him along the Mediterranean, providing a rare opportunity for the friends to catch up on the past 16 years.

"It was wonderful," Frank said. "But it still wasn't enough. Nothing we say or do can ever fill the spaces between our lives."

Another day Margit and Frank teamed up with Miriam and Kurt and two other couples for an excursion to Eilat and the Red Sea. They drove through the desert and around two large craters, each perhaps half a mile in diameter and equally as deep.

"We drove around and around on rough terrain. The other car, a Jeep, had no trouble," Frank said. "But our four-cylinder engine, maybe the size of a sewing machine, became overheated. We were stuck."

There were no gas stations, no garages. The only person they found was an Arab willing to help. Without much confidence, Frank rolled the car into the man's tent on the sand and watched as he took apart the engine. Every screw, piston, valve and piece of metal was laid out on Arab newspapers in the sun.

"I was sure we would be there for days," Frank said. "With all my engineering schooling I couldn't accomplish what this man did in one day without a machine shop and without sophisticated tools. Thanks to him we could bring our car back to London and then the United States."

Before Frank and Margit left Israel, Frank's father arranged for one of his clients to invite them to dinner. Mr. Milkowski bought refrigeration equipment for Israeli ice cream factories. He also enjoyed special respect within the community because his son was mayor of Tel Aviv.

"In between hummus and pita bread we talked about refrigeration equipment," Frank said. "After roast chicken and *babaganush* we reviewed his plans for expansion. By the time his wife served dessert, Mr. Milkowski offered me a job as an engineer in his plant. Which country was to be my home, Israel or America, was no longer a philosophical discussion. I now had a real opportunity."

Margit agreed to stay in Israel or move back to Los Angeles. It was all up to Frank. What to do?

"I had no job waiting for me in America," Frank said. "My family lived on the East Coast and I planned to live on the West Coast so even if we went back to the States I wouldn't see my parents or my cousins often. I always make lists of pros and cons then consider them for a long time. I created a long list. Then I jotted down a short list. Afterward I tore up both lists and went with my intuition. I decided to go back but I can't tell you why. Maybe I had already made my commitment to America when I became a naturalized citizen. I only know it felt good to return by choice."

Frank and Margit settled into a two-bedroom apartment in Los Angeles on Hollywood Boulevard near Laurel Canyon. It had white furniture and a white rug. Max liked it so much he bought the whole building. Later Frank and Margit invested in a house in Sherman Oaks on Woodman Drive.

"I think the orange tree in the backyard and the jacaranda that bloomed blue flowers every spring convinced me this was the place for us, that California was my place for life," Frank said.

23: Finding a Career

1964   *Start of a long period of relative peace between East*
       and West following resolution of the Cuban Missile
       Crisis.

       The Beatles are featured on the Ed Sullivan Show.

1965   *A failing economy in Czechoslovakia led communist*
       leaders to encourage industrial development with
       new trading partners.

Margit's father wanted Frank to join his company, Ponder
& Best, a camera-importing firm that was later renamed
Vivitar. Frank and Max had endless discussions until Frank
finally agreed, ready to plant some roots. The company
occupied a one-story office building. Their warehouse was
in back, close to the Desi Arnaz studio.

"We used to eat lunch in a nearby restaurant where I
often saw Dick Van Dyke."

"Did you see other celebrities?" I asked.

Frank shrugged. "Maybe. I don't know actors
unless you're sitting next to me to point them out," he said.
"I was busy concentrating on my work."

Max was tough. He told everyone what he thought even if the words stung. His brother-in-law and business partner, John Best, was smooth as oil. John would say lovely things, but you never knew what he was thinking, which direction the oil would flow. The two men would close the door to their adjoining offices and yell at each other. None of the 20 or so workers could make out what they said but the arguments were awful. John was in charge of purchasing and Max handled sales. If the supply and demand didn't match, each blamed the other for not doing his task properly.

"I disregarded their disputes," Frank said. "They were family and I thought it was more important to work for Max than for a stranger. I was wrong."

In true *yekke* style, both Max and John believed Frank should start at the bottom.

"My first assignment was to broom the warehouse," he said.

"You mean with all your education and experience you were asked to sweep?"

"I also packaged orders," he said.

"In the mailroom?"

"Right. I was out of college seven years—seven years of engineering experience. I kept telling them they weren't using my skills."

At first the partners ignored Frank. Then they moved him to the import department under John where Frank ordered cameras and lenses from Japan. Later he wrote follow up letters to suppliers.

"If I stayed, Frank said, "it was clear I would be wasting many years, but Max was my father-in-law. How could I quit?"

Frank wrote a letter to Max and John asking for more responsibilities. With Margit's and her mother's approval he told them that if these requests were not met within a year, he would leave.

"They didn't believe me," Frank said.

By 1963 Margit and Frank's first son, Michael, was born. Frank's grandmother, Marta, flew out from New York to help for two months and his parents often visited. At one point during a walk, Frank's father asked him to join his company in New York. His mom already worked with his dad and this would make it a complete family operation specializing in importing textile machinery.

"I understood machines and I knew about sales," Frank said. "This was my chance to depart from Ponder & Best in a nice way and to be my own boss."

Margit was delighted to leave the glitz of Los Angeles and Hollywood, to move to Larchmont where Frank had spent his first days in America when he stayed with Uncle Herbert and Aunt Stella.

"It was a perfect place to start the next chapter in our lives," Frank said.

"If you are to sell machines, you need to meet the people we represent," Frank's father said before sending him and his family to Europe in 1965. "Selling machinery is not like selling a camera. It is a long process. You start by finding out what your customer expects to produce. This determines the type of equipment he will buy. For example, how many spindles or winding machines will he need and how will they fit together. It will be up to you to help calculate the building specs to the inch and make sure they fit onto the floor space in the customer's factory."

His dad designed a three-month apprenticeship with his suppliers. All the companies were family-owned businesses with grown sons who worked for their fathers. Each specialized in one or two segments of the total textile manufacturing process.

"I had seen many of these steps during my summer in Canada," Frank said. "I thought I knew it all—starting with cotton or wool or synthetic fiber, cleaning and then lining up the raw material using a carding machine. I had worked with equipment that made yarn ready for dyeing or weaving or knitting. What more did I need to be a good salesman? I felt like I was doing my father a favor by going to Europe."

Since Frank spoke German the first stop was Georg Sahm GmbH & Co. in Eschwege, Germany east of Frankfurt. During his four-week stint he rotated from manufacturing to sales and marketing.

"Sahm precision winding machines took endless streams of fiber and wound them onto giant spools of thread, maybe one hundred times bigger than my grandmother's spools for mending," Frank said. "I was so impressed I bought six machines without consulting my dad and before any client had ordered one."

His father was furious. Normally their company only requested what they presold. Fred was worried they would be stuck with the equipment. But Frank believed in this new technology. It could control the exact weight of a four-ounce pull skein for hand knitting yarns so every bundle of yarn would weigh the same.

"I knew that the Caron Spinning Company in Rochelle, Illinois, was looking for such consistency," Frank said. "They bought all six machines."

This was the first time Frank and Margit lived in Germany. A short time into his apprenticeship Frank could add numbers in German instead of translating first. The couple became totally immersed in the lifestyle and decided to speak German to their son so that he, too, would learn the language.

"The weirdest thing is that we started to dream in German," Frank said. "Everything felt familiar."

Frank also became close friends with Reiner Wassman, the Sales Manager at Sahm. Margit spent much time with Reiner's wife who showed her how to cook pork and fry *wienerschnitzel* and which beer was best for *weisswurst*, a sausage made from veal and fresh pork bacon. On one of their excursions they were so close to the German East/West border Frank and Margit could see the military Watch Towers through binoculars.

"The young soldiers looked like boys carrying huge guns," Frank said. "I never saw them smile and I wondered how many people they had shot trying to escape to the West. When I saw those Watch Towers, I was grateful to be an American."

After one month Frank and Margit and Michael moved east of Brussels to Aalst, Belgium, where Frank worked for Gilbos, makers of textile machines. The workers' main language was Flemish so Frank had to communicate in English, which was more challenging than his previous experience in Germany. He had a sweet tooth and it didn't take long for him to develop a craving for the very thin chocolate that was molded to look like the bark of a tree.

"The Gilbos plant was huge with 200 employees. They produced random winding machines using a high-speed technology that wound yarns with minimal hairiness," Frank said.

"Hairiness? What are you talking about?" I asked not able to imagine a carding or precision or random winding machine.

"At Gilbos the spun fibers varied in length, no more than four inches long. Since they were diverse they could not be spun perfectly and therefore kept some fuzz, called hair. The fuzz is similar to what you see in woven upholstery fabric as well as carpet tufting."

In Belgium Frank and Margit stayed in a hotel within walking distance from the factory. First he was placed with the sales team. He sat in on meetings to determine the production of the equipment and what alterations were needed to increase speed and satisfy client's requests.

"This was new to me," Frank said. "Every buyer had a different size factory and floor space and wanted to produce a different end product. That meant each machine had to be customized. My engineering background was critical. With buyers investing thousands of dollars for a line of equipment, risk was high. We had to figure out how much they needed to sell to recoup their investment and make a profit. For the first time in my apprenticeship I understood why my father had sent me overseas."

On the days he was assigned to the factory Frank wore a smock just like the other workers who wanted to keep oil and dust off their clothes. With plaid shirts peeking out from heavy navy or gray sweaters, beautiful warm scarves and the most fashionable glasses, the workers resembled men at leisure rather than engineers and craftsmen welding metal in one hundred different ways. Despite ceilings that were two stories high, the factory always smelled as if something were burning. The sound of drilling bounced off the walls creating an echo.

Frank ate lunch with the management team in a restaurant and he and Margit were welcomed for dinner at the home of one of the two Gilbos brothers who owned the company. One brother, Paul, had ten children.

"He and his wife sat on opposite ends of the table in their kitchen with five kids, ranging from three to 18, on each side of the table." Frank said. "I usually sat near Mrs. Gilbos enjoying mussels cooked in beer. The kids all drank beer, even the very young ones. At a certain point a stranger walked in and sat on the other side of Mrs. Gilbos. Later I was told he was her boyfriend."

Paul said, "If it makes my wife happy, I'm happy."

Frank already knew this attitude. When Paul had visited in Larchmont, they watched TV one evening. Paul put his arm around Margit and tried to seduce her, claiming it would make all of them happy.

"Margit almost threw him out of the house," Frank said. "Still, seeing Mrs. Gilbos with her husband and her boyfriend was an uncomfortable surprise."

Frank's last month was with the Carniti Company in Oggiono, Italy, 40 kilometers northeast of Milan near Lecco. Dario Carniti lived in a fancy villa with a swimming pool and view of the mountains. He had three kids. His wife, Maria, arranged elaborate meals. Waiters wore white gloves and served elegant dinners in their formal dining room. Mr. Carniti dressed in fine-tailored Italian suits and woven silk ties. His shoes always looked new.

"He sent his driver and Jaguar to Milano to pick us up at the airport," Frank said.

That was just his business car. Personally, he drove a Lamborghini, a high-speed tomato red Miura two-seater. He was the biggest employer in the town and owned a hotel near the factory where his clients stayed.

"In the village he was greeted like a king," Frank said. "When he took us to the best restaurants people stood to welcome him. One time I accepted a ride in his sports car. He drove 100 miles an hour through tiny streets. The buildings on each side had front doors that opened onto the road. I was sure we would hit someone who happened to leave an apartment when we flew by. Years later I heard that Dario had driven with a friend from Milano to Roma in two separate but similar Lamborghini Miura two-seaters. Along the way, his friend missed a curve and tumbled off a mountain. The car and driver were never found. Dario sold his car."

At work Carniti built spinning frames incorporating a technology from the wool industry. The result was a beautiful smooth yarn for carpets. With every frame requiring 25 feet by 50 feet, the installations were huge.

"Imagine a four-car garage and you have an idea of how much floor space was needed," Frank said. "Each frame then used 152 spindles to produce packages of yarn."

In later years Carniti flew to Burlington Industries with Frank and together they sold over 258 of these machines that were installed in five facilities in America as well as Japan and Germany. On one of their trips Carniti met a stewardess at a bar in New York, a red-haired German woman who worked for Lufthansa. The next day he told Frank he was in love, totally smitten. Three years later he divorced his wife and married the German girl. They stayed together for the rest of his life.

Carniti received many orders for complete lines of cotton spinning frames. To fulfill the demand from the Far East he decided to expand. Through Frank, he bought 500 used carding machines that had been updated at the John D. Hollingsworth factory in Greenville, South Carolina.

"I think the three-month apprenticeship was among my most exciting times of my life," Frank said. "I learned machinery. I perfected my English and picked up some Italian. Margit and I experienced three countries while developing new friendships."

"So at Gilbos you learned about open marriage as well as random winding machines," I said. "At Carniti you learned about secret infidelity, divorce and speeding as well as spinning machines. But at Sahm, the German company, everything was perfect, right?" I asked.

"Of course," Frank said.

24: Selling Machines From Czechoslovakia

*1946-1989   Eastern Bloc of communist countries
    participates in the Cold War.*

*1947   Czechoslovakia aligns with communist countries
    behind the Iron Curtain.*

1968   Warsaw Pact forces invade Czechoslovakia.

Frank's next assignment was to attend international textile machinery exhibitions where textile manufacturers view the newest equipment and renew relationships with suppliers and customers. The shows are held once every four years in European cities that have enough convention space to house acres of machinery. From making fibers, to weaving to pressing and stitching nonwovens, the shows encompass a cornucopia of opportunities for entrepreneurs.

"My parents and I walked and walked, visiting at least five or seven buildings per day, some with lines of machines the size of a hotel ballroom," Frank said. "Mother always wore her heels no matter how many hours we walked."

The shows attracted thousands of visitors and featured equipment from all over the world including Communist countries that were not allowed to do business in the United States.

At one show Frank's father discovered the Arachne machine that was developed by engineers in Czechoslovakia, probably at the government-owned Institute for Nonwovens. The Czech equipment produced nonwoven cloth at three times the speed of a loom. This technology was perfect for manufacturing blankets, towels and baby pajamas. By setting up smaller factories and using less electricity, entrepreneurs could make a substantial profit.

Fred decided to bring the Arachne to America. He reached out to Dr. Alois Marek, the sales rep from Investa that sold the Arachne. Dr. Marek agreed to work with him and to sell the machines to manufacturers in the United States even though Czechoslovakia was Communist at that time and the government, the Czech Soviet Socialist Republic, owned or controlled everything including Investa.

Back in America Fred obtained permission to import the Czech equipment. He then introduced the Arachne to the Beacon Manufacturing Company in Swannanoa, North Carolina, the biggest blanket maker in the world. They bought 20 of these machines.

A few years later, in 1968 or 1969, Frank flew to Czechoslovakia to meet with Dr. Marek. They were the same age. They each had two sons and a friendship bloomed despite political differences. At that time the Communists didn't allow foreigners to fraternize with the Czechs, but Al invited Frank home anyway.

"He took me there after dark," Frank said. "Al's father and mother had lived in the house for many years.

146

When the Communists took over they divided the house into five apartments. Al and Mary and their two sons shared one of those apartments."

"Was Al afraid his neighbors would see you and tell someone?" I asked.

"I don't know," Frank said shrugging his shoulders. "Al told me to keep quiet until we were inside. He kept the lights low and the curtains drawn, but most East Europeans did that anyway."

Mary had gone to the butcher at 5:00 a.m. to buy whatever was available. She prepared meat and dumplings with a heavy brown sauce. "I don't know how long she saved to pay for it," Frank said, "but I left a few American dollars that Al hid."

When Frank and Al traveled to other Czech manufacturing plants, in addition to beautiful fields and forests, Frank could see a number of watchtowers placed along the Czech and West German border. The big black car they were using emphasized the drama especially since the driver from Investa listened to their conversation.

"It sounds like a James Bond thriller," I said.

"If you say so," Frank said.

Al was not a member of the Communist party, but he was one of Holub's sales agents and Mr. Holub was a member of the party. Holub was the director at the Arachne factory. Holub invited Al and Frank to the Arachne company *dacha* (country home) in the forest. There were no other houses in the area. Inside, the walls were paneled in dark wood and lined with stuffed heads of animals.

"Boar with long teeth, deer with big brown eyes and bucks with large horns seemed to stare at me," Frank said.

Holub and Frank drank giant glasses of Pilsner beer, perhaps a quart per person. Frank sat next to a plant so he could dump his drink into the soil when nobody was looking. Holub demanded Frank join him in a brotherly dance on the table to symbolize their friendship. Their arms were interlocked while they each held foaming glasses of beer. Later Holub gave Frank a piece of art—two clowns made of yarns stitched together on the Arachne machine. Holub signed the art.

"Was he implying that you are both clowns caught in different political webs?" I asked.

"I don't know," Frank said while taking a Pilsner from our refrigerator. "We never discussed politics, religion, capitalism or communism. He was a big party member and I was far from home. There were many rules restricting personal activities in Czechoslovakia, including a law that prohibited the removal of art, so I hid the art in my suitcase and later hung it in my office."

While Frank worked with the Czechs he heard stories of some people who were able to escape during the Communist regime. Mike Vavra, Al's boss, was very clever. He showed Frank books with homemade covers stuffed with U.S. dollars, British pounds and German marks. Later he unscrewed the inside panel of his car door to stash his international money.

"On my next visit I heard that Mike Vavra had escaped," Frank said.

Al and Mary, along with Vavra, his wife and daughters had driven to the border to vacation nearby. Vavra convinced the guard at the checkpoint near Italy that he wanted his wife to eat real Italian pasta. They let him through because he was a high-ranking official at Investa. Vavra then drove to Munich to the American Embassy to seek political asylum. Somehow he was able to send his two daughters to America and later asked the Americans to allow him and his wife to join them to keep his family together.

"All four got out," Frank said, "and I helped him find a home in Queens and a job in New York."

When Al and Mary returned to their house, the Communists interrogated Al. They demanded to know if he had known about Vavra's plan, or, worse, was part of the scheme. Fortunately, Al was able to talk his way out of the dilemma.

Another time Al asked Frank to bring a Kodak slide projector to Prague. Instead of concealing it in an unmarked package, Frank carried it in its original container. When he arrived at the Prague airport, the customs officer marked Frank's passport indicating he had brought in a Kodak projector. That meant Frank had to take it out when he left.

Determined to keep the gift, Al gave Frank the original box filled with textile samples.

"Al and his friend, another member of the Communist party, came with us to the airport," Frank said. "Al chatted with the customs official while I checked in. His friend put my Kodak box and luggage on the conveyor belt. By the time the official noticed my passport he saw the box leaving and gave me clearance by stamping my passport."

"What could have happened to you if you were caught?" I asked.

"Don't ask me such questions," Frank said with a laugh. "I would have told them I brought the samples with me in that box. You have to think fast, be quick, not hem and haw."

On other trips he brought home Jewish memorabilia he had bought secretly from someone at the Alt Neu Shul, the Old New Synagogue in Prague and one of the oldest in Europe. Many artifacts from throughout Eastern Europe were collected there. For his synagogue in Larchmont, Frank bought an eternal light and a silver pointer used to read the torah because according to Orthodox laws, one is not allowed to touch the parchment.

Frank loved paintings, drawings and sculpture. He used to take his sons to museums and bribed his Michael with a nickel for every artist Michael could name when they visited exhibits. In addition to Holub's clown present Frank was determined to bring home another piece of art from Czechoslovakia. The problem was that artists could not sell their work privately.

Though it was dangerous, Frank bought tapestries made from knotted yarn by a well-known artist named Luba Krejci. Luba and her husband removed her work from its frame, balled it up and handed it to Frank to stuff inside his laundry in his suitcase. On his next trip he brought Luba a lens for her son's camera and Frank later arranged for her to have an exhibit in New York City. Two pieces of Luba's art now hang in our living room.

Frank's favorite story about Czechoslovakia concerns his client who owned a weaving mill in Massachusetts. He and his wife joined Frank and 21 other Americans to tour a number of factories in Prague. The client's wife was more than uncomfortable. She was scared. Frank tried to convince her this would be an informative and enjoyable experience. Then came the bus. It had been built in Eastern Europe and looked solid. But the roads were narrow, one-lane passageways. An army convoy was moving slowly in front of them. Their driver zigzagged in between the military vehicles, trying to pass as many as he could.

"I recall the trucks carried missiles," Frank said. "They were so huge that when I looked out the bus my face was at the same level as the tires."

At a certain moment the bus squeezed between two trucks. As it passed it smashed into the truck's bumper and knocked off the front side of the bus, unraveling the entire outside paneling on the right side. The client's wife was in shock.

"We all were," Frank said. "But we continued our journey, glad it wasn't raining since we were pretty much out in the open air. I was happy Margit was safe at home, a Cub Scout den mother baking cakes."

On another trip Frank observed traditional machines that line up fibers in a parallel so the fibers could be twisted together. The machines could blend two different fibers, perhaps fine cotton from Egypt with less expensive, less perfect cotton. This system is still popular.

"In The Cotton Research Center in Usti nad Orlici, about 150 kilometers southeast of Prague, the Czechs designed a new, smaller blending technology called the BD-200. Production became three times faster and used less factory space and less electricity. Frank obtained special permission from both governments to import and sell the machinery in the USA.

"It revolutionized the industry," Frank said. "We sold many of these open-end spinning machines. Americans opened factories along the rivers up and down the East Coast and created lots of jobs. It was a prosperous time for everyone."

25: Many Losses

1966   Indira Gandhi is elected Prime Minister of India.

*1968   Martin Luther King, Jr. and Robert F. Kennedy are
assassinated.*

In 1966 Frank's second child, David Haldon, was born in
New York. The newborn had a growth the size of a small
orange that was lodged against his intestine and blocked
circulation of his blood. He needed an operation.

Frank's dad had scheduled a business meeting in
Europe followed by a quick stop in Israel to attend the
wedding of his distant cousin, Gidi. When Fred realized the
newborn was at risk, he wanted to cancel his trip to be with
Frank. The family convinced him to go anyway. After Fred
left, the baby developed an infection and needed to be
opened up again. The baby did not survive the second
operation.

"I never knew my son," Frank said. "I watched him
through a glass wall. Our infant never came home from the
hospital. He didn't have a chance to experience the future
we all hoped to share. It was terrible, but I think it was even
worse for Margit."

Frank called his dad who had just returned to his hotel after hiking with a client on Zugspitze, the tallest mountain in Germany near the Austrian border. His father changed his plans to come right home. On the flight from Berlin to Frankfurt Fred had a heart attack. Hilda immediately bought a ticket to be with him but her passport had expired.

"I raced to Rockefeller Center in Manhattan to get it renewed," Frank said. "My sister claims she was the one who went to Rockefeller Center."

Hilda rushed to Germany to be with her husband the day he was to check out of the hospital. Coincidentally, Frank's Uncle Herbert and Aunt Stella were in Switzerland and flew to be with him in Frankfurt. Fred seemed to be recovering. While Hilda planned a two-week rest in Switzerland, Fred found time to dictate some thoughts he wanted Hilda to share with Frank and Ada. He said:

> Always require intellectual honesty and begin with yourself. Permit no one, including yourself, to get involved with duplicity. To win, you must face reality as it is—not as you wish it to be—and you must face it on a sound ethical basis. Invest a great amount of time in good men. Live and think with them—dream with them.
>
> Your work must have a meaning to you and you should know the final result and goal. Learn to disagree without being offensive. Do not needle people and do not be ironical. Learn how to draw out people without being indiscreet. Learn to be forceful without being domineering. Learn to avoid passing your own anxiety on to others. Try to think before arguing. Everyone should have his own self-education program that should

include avid reading in your professional business but also in other fields.

You cannot always get the optimum out of life. Do not ask what others are doing, but have your own approach to people. Never be negative. Be yourself and do not pretend.

Perhaps Fred had a premonition when he wrote his message because within two weeks after his first heart attack, he suffered a second massive heart attack and died.

"The loss of my father was devastating for me," Frank said.

"I understand," I said, remembering my father who died after my freshman year at college. Lung cancer. Three packs a day. He'd always tried to get me to smoke. My brother was about to turn 15. It was hard for my mother, but she stepped up and took over his drugstore and put us through college without any debt."

"It was hardest for my mom, too," Frank said, "yet she never snapped."

Earlier that year she had held her mother, *omi* Marta, in her arms when *omi* died of pneumonia. *Omi* was 86. The family loved her and missed her, but it is part of life for the elder generation to pass first. Frank's dad was 62, much too young.

"I couldn't help but wonder," Frank said, "maybe I shouldn't have told him about the baby until he came home. Maybe the stress caused his heart attack."

Frank's mother wouldn't hear such nonsense. She wouldn't let him waste time comparing which loss was worse.

"They were all bad," she told Frank. "Comfort your wife and son. Try to remember the positive things and gather the strength to go forward."

Frank missed his dad. He remembered as a kid watching him sit in their little dinette, accounting income versus cost of living, trying not to spend money, never overextending himself.

"He taught me to be happy with less," Frank said. "When he died, I felt cheated because I only got to work with him for two years. He knew the textile industry and had so much more to teach me."

Frank's father left him and his mother as co-owners and co-workers of the company, Stellamcor, Inc. Sometimes it went well. She could add columns of numbers faster than he could read them. Typing on a typewriter with two fingers she could complete 100 memos and letters in one day. Other times Frank was angry at his father for leaving him with her, making him assume many financial and social responsibilities that should have been his dad's. Ada and her family lived in Oak Ridge, Tennessee, so taking mother to restaurants, driving together to family events and traveling overseas with her to international textile machinery shows fell to Frank.

"She knew everyone in the industry," Frank said. "When I went to meetings without her, people always asked me, 'How is your mother?'"

Since Frank's mother lived alone in the Bronx, he sold the house and moved her to an apartment in Larchmont that was a short walk from their house and near the train station to Manhattan. She still loved wearing heels and elegant suits and enjoyed making friends on the train to the office, especially one gentleman who spoke French with her.

"Life was settling into a nice routine," Frank said. "I wanted to enjoy our Michael and move forward as a small family, but Margit wanted another baby."

"I was so worried because by now we knew that Margit's blood had an Rh negative factor and mine was positive," Frank said.

The mismatch meant trouble that usually kicks in after the first pregnancy. Their baby, their third fetus, inherited Frank's Rh-positive factor. Margit's body treated the baby as a foreign substance and started to reject him. At birth the baby became anemic and needed transfusions. But this time medical assistance worked and David Fredrick Levy came home.

"It was a bit of a miracle," I said, thinking about David and my son, Michael, becoming friends when they were eight and later, inadvertently, bringing Frank and me together.

Things seemed to be looking brighter when Margit got pregnant a fourth time but this baby died in utero. It never had a name.

26: Satisfied In Suburbia

1969   July 20: Man lands on the moon.

*1974   The World Trade Organization agreement on textiles
and clothing provides for gradual dismantlement of
quotas that limit Third World exports to developed
countries.*

*The Trade Act of 1974 signed to help U.S.
manufacturers become more competitive.*

For many years Frank and Margit led a blessed life. They
lived in a charming Tudor house with a 22-foot beamed
ceiling and a stone fireplace in the living room. Michael
and David enjoyed their own rooms. The house had three
bathrooms upstairs, a spare room with a window in the attic
and enough closets to hang up their clothes without old-
fashioned armoires. Frank could walk into town or to the
train station to catch the 7:32 to his office in Manhattan.

Though Uncle Herbert and a group of his friends
had founded a reform synagogue in Larchmont, Margit and
Frank opted to join a smaller, conservative synagogue
down the block where most of the services were in Hebrew.

"I thought my children would learn Hebrew better there than at a reformed temple," Frank said.

They were part of a small group, about 150 families. Margit became treasurer of the Women's Division and eventually Frank took over the Presidency.

"I know some people criticize suburbia, even laugh at the provincial choice of lifestyle," Frank said. "But ordinary days gave me peace and balanced my heavy travel overseas. The boys attended school and Margit enjoyed being a full-time mom."

On weekends Frank coached David's soccer team and helped his sons learn to ride their bikes. Michael was a great swimmer and they were all expert skiers. They were involved in the community and the local synagogue and did most things suburban families do.

"I liked my routine. I thrived knowing that each day could be the same as the day before. I had found my forever place to plant my feet."

Meanwhile, Frank's business was growing. Each client demanded customized equipment to produce different end products. To help calculate their requirements and fill orders Frank needed three secretaries and more space. He moved his company from 43rd Street to a larger place at 331 Madison Avenue. Being a *yekke*, Frank liked to hold meetings without business correspondence or files in sight so he also rented a conference room with a table that could seat 10 people.

"It was an expansive, elegant environment and my first investment in building an image," Frank said.

Confident about their future, they bought a small ski house in the Berkshires and taught their boys to ski at Jiminy Peak. It had one chair lift. At the base of the mountain was a simple building. They used to bring lunch and meet other families there. Sometimes the owner sat with them. One time he asked a few of the regulars to each invest $5,000 or $10,000 to build up the resort.

"I was happy to help the fledgling resort grow," Frank said. "In exchange our family received free skiing for life, which turned out to be a great deal."

As the boys grew older they brought all their friends to ski. At night they would relax in the hot tub then spread sleeping bags on the floor.

Frank and his family loved Jiminy Peak. But they were expert skiers and sometimes sought more demanding slopes. Frank took his family to the Peruvian Lodge in Alta, Utah, for a more challenging experience. They liked it because it wasn't fancy: just simple chair lifts and well-packed snow to slide down in the most natural setting.

Of course, twice a year they visited Margit's family in the West. They combined the reunion with a ski trip to Mammouth Mountain Resort in northern California.

"One summer break we took Michael and David on their first trip to Israel. By then Chezzi had four children around the same age as our boys. Michael joined Chezzi's oldest son, Yuval, in Boy Scout camp for a day or two. During our trip Michael had his bar mitzvah at the Western Wall in Jerusalem."

The family also drove to Eilat with a group arranged by a kibbutz that owned large vehicles able to drive through mountains and desert. The wheels were about 8-feet in diameter. They slept in sleeping bags under the stars at the foothills of Mt. Sinai."

"Early the next morning we hiked to the top of the mountain where Moses had received the Ten Commandments." Frank said. "I often referred to this trip when we skied in Zürs/St. Anton, Zermatt, Vermont, Utah and Colorado. When we came back from Israel I couldn't have been happier."

Then came the hard part. In 1978 Dario Carniti, Frank's biggest supplier of spinning machinery, went bankrupt. Carniti did not get his final payments for machines he had sold to companies in the Far East. Italian labor laws had dictated that Carniti provide a three-course lunch every day for his 1,200 employees. With no money coming in to fund these lunches and no income to cover business expenses, he was pushed into bankruptcy.

"I felt terrible for him," Frank said. "I had two orders for spinning frames from companies in Canada. I needed to find another supplier. It was a disaster and I didn't know what would come next, but I was open to all possibilities and that's when my biggest business break emerged."

27: A Shift To Recycling

1966   The Red Guard demonstrates in China against Western influences.

1978   The People's Republic of China opens for foreign investment

Deng Xiaoping leads the Communist Party of China.

When Frank joined his parents' company in the mid-1960s, numerous textile mills lined the rivers in New England. He sold Carniti's machines to a division of Burlington Industries in North Carolina, as well as to Avondale Mills and Beacon Manufacturing in Georgia. These Southern companies provided jobs to people who lived in the Black Mountains and Appalachia. Owners did so well that they supported universities, recreation centers and town projects. Some even provided housing for employees.

"It was a prosperous time for us and for America," Frank said. "One of my favorite clients, Johnny Glidden, owned a second generation woolen mill in Vermont, along a river that provided energy where he created his own electricity. The company made woolen yarn and sold it to manufacturers in New York who then made coats and skirts."

In 1978 the United States began diplomatic relations with the People's Republic of China. Exchange rates favored developed countries and foreign investors started to pump money into China.

"I didn't pay attention to the new laws that were created," Frank said. "I didn't realize American companies would shift their domestic production from local mills to countries that paid lower wages. Who could blame them? Labor was cheaper in Asia. If companies manufactured overseas, they could make a bigger profit. The change didn't happen right away. It took five to 10 years for my clients to stop buying our machines."

With the new trade laws, countries with lower hourly wages could import fibers and textile waste from America. They manufactured clothing, then shipped the garments back at a cheaper price than goods made in the USA. The textile manufacturing industry in the United States started to close down. Many American mills closed. Some relocated to Texas and California where they could acquire cotton fiber without trucking expenses.

The Beacon Manufacturing Company once sold an estimated 21 million blankets per year. They were the largest producers of blankets in America. By 2002 they closed their plant in Swannanoa, North Carolina. Hundreds of workers who lived in the Appalachian Mountains lost their jobs. Cannon Mills once dominated the towel and sheet industries. Slowly they also downsized. In 2003 they went bankrupt.

"Over the years," Frank said, "I think hundreds of factories in North Carolina alone were put up for sale. Thousands of people were out of work. Today many of these factories along the length of the Coast are boarded up."

"Like the abandoned old Bulova Watch Company in Sag Harbor, not far from where we live on Long Island," I said.

Others have found new uses. The Massachusetts Museum of Contemporary Art (MASS MoCA) inhabits numerous old red brick textile factory buildings in North Adams, Massachusetts. Other factories have been turned into old age homes or apartments.

"It became harder for my friend, Johnny Glidden, to compete." Frank said.

Glidden couldn't pay his domestic workers a fair wage and sell his woolen yarn at a price that was as cheap as Chinese-made goods. He sold his company to a firm in China.

"Imagine there are no woolen mills in America now. I think they all closed," Frank said. "It's the plight of our country that we allowed manufacturing to shift to China and Mexico. We need to restart manufacturing right here in the USA. We need our young people to become engineers. Maybe if there were fancy award shows for innovative engineering instead of just for acting or singing young people would gravitate to engineering. Maybe they'd use their creative spark to solve this problem."

While China was quietly building up its textile production capabilities, Frank shifted from selling machinery that made yarn to also sell machinery that recycled textiles and textile waste.

Frank turned to Carniti's competitor, Franco Conti, at SACFEM in Arezzo. In addition to spinning machines, SACFEM made a 100-inch-wide Garnett machine that opened spun textile waste back into fiber utilizing metal wires like the teeth of a comb. The equipment used big cylinders that operated at a high speed.

"Each Garnett machine weighed about four tons or more, maybe as much as two cars. When they ran, they had to be accurate from edge to edge. There was no margin for error," Frank said. "To sell Garnetts would be another shift in my career. I'd have to cultivate a new set of potential buyers, but something compelled me to explore the possibility."

Schiapparelli, the engineer who had designed the Garnett, drove Frank to Prato outside of Florence to watch his machine in action. While Frank wandered around the plant, fate intervened. He spotted a similar machine with a production rate that was even five times faster. Schiapparelli was disappointed because he realized Frank would not sell SACFEM's Garnetts.

The man who emerged from that area of the factory had particles of fiber and dust clinging to his navy blue work clothes. His fingers were coated in grease. Schiapparelli asked the man to explain the technology to Frank. The man grabbed a handful of finished fiber from the machine, kissed it and threw it back.

"Tell the American he's too rich to understand the value of this technology," he said in Italian. "Americans like to throw everything away. We Italians prefer to recycle all waste."

Schiapparelli translated and Frank could feel his Palestinian dream of saving the land bubbling up from another time. He could taste the importance of reusing what we have, not just in the mid-East or Europe or America, but in all parts of our planet. Frank looked at Schiapperelli.

"Do you know who built this machine?" he asked. "I never saw anything like it. I need to talk to the person who designed this machine."

"Yes," Schiapparelli said. "But it is late."

"Please, you must take me to him now," Frank said.

Prato has been the center of the textile industry since medieval days. Old clothes and other textile waste are brought to the city from all over the world then transformed back into fiber for knitting or weaving fashionable clothing and beautiful fabrics. Most machine manufacturers in Prato specialize in building machines that recycle textile waste.

"I had never been interested in meeting anyone in Prato," Frank said. "Many of the companies in that area are small, family-owned businesses. I sold to large companies that usually needed lots of machines from big suppliers. But this machine was special."

When Frank pulled up in front of the Dell'Orco & Villani factory, Sergio had his heavy metal key in his hand about to lock up before joining his family for dinner in their upstairs apartment.

"We talked," Frank said. "Sergio explained that his technology is used to create blended new fibers out of old clothes and raw materials for nonwovens."

"Like felt," I said.

"Exactly," Frank said, "and under padding for carpets, insulation for automobiles, wiping cloths and blankets like the Mormons or Red Cross distribute during emergencies. I told Sergio I was ready to represent his "green" technology in North America if he was ready to be my next machine supplier."

They shook hands and when they parted Frank carried an eight-millimeter film about Sergio's process. Later the two men partnered to design a variety of technologies in the textile machinery industry that would also save the land.

"Schiaparelli and I also became friends for years," Frank said.

At home Frank checked the Davison Textile Blue Book, the annual directory for all aspects of the industry, where he found 50 businesses that processed textile waste. Hilda wrote to them and within a week a company in Upstate New York invited Frank to Broadalbin, Northwest of Albany, New York. Frank showed the owner, David Kissinger, the film he carried along with his Kodak projector. After the screening, David gave Frank a tour of his factory. It was a mess of old machinery with lots of fiber flying all over. There weren't enough safety mechanisms.

"Well, what do you think?" Kissinger asked.

"I told him the truth," Frank said. "He was much taller, so I looked up and told him I thought he would go bankrupt. His old-fashioned Garnett machines were only 40-inches wide with a production of 50-80 pounds of mixed fibers per hour."

Frank invited Kissinger to Italy.

"If you see nothing new or of interest," he said, "I'll pay for your trip."

Kissinger and his wife flew to Prato. He bought the first 60-inch wide opening machine that could produce about 1,000 pounds of mixed fibers per hour.

"Imagine a giant boa constrictor swallowing up a pile of small pieces of clothing," Frank said, "and spitting them out as fibers. That's how our machine worked."

Later Kissinger bought 20 more cylinders, blenders, boxes and cutters, becoming Frank's first big textile-recycling customer.

"Where did your customers get their textile waste?" I asked.

"Mills, production waste, tailor's clips and used clothing," Frank said.

When people donate garments to places like the Salvation Army or churches, the clothes are sorted then sold by the pound to locals or Third World countries. Articles in bad condition are sold by the pound to companies in the fiber opening business.

"How does fiber opening work?" I asked.

"A cutting machine cuts the clothes into small pieces, maybe 20 inches by 20 inches," Frank said. "A second cutting machine re-cuts the pieces at right angles. The pieces, called clips, are fed to a blending box machine that is the size of a trailer. From there the material goes into an opening machine, six cylinders at a time adding up to 100 feet long. Next the opened fibers are fed into a press to make 500-pound bales before being shipped to a nonwoven plant that makes blankets or wipes or other end products."

"Isn't there still something left at the end?" I asked.

"Everything gets used and reused," Frank said. "Even the waste of the waste gets cleaned and opened to make padding to be used under carpets or for heat and sound insulation panels. These fibers are called a blend of 1,000 flowers."

One of Frank's clients in California used to purchase old clothes. He employed maybe 400 people to sort and disperse the goods to different countries. It was a very profitable business—enough for him to afford his own jet plane. Still, there was much waste. "Through Sergio we met in Manhattan," Frank said. "Based on a handshake, we designed a turnkey recycling plant for the man. Before he bought Sergio's machines, he dumped the unusable pieces into landfills, maybe two truckloads every day. With the new machinery he helped to reduce waste in some landfills, provided jobs and made a profit."

28: Hugs And Tears

1971   President Nixon signs the National Cancer Act.

1980s The breast cancer movement develops out of larger feminist efforts, especially those associated women's health initiatives.

Frank had successfully reinvented himself. Life was whole again. Then Margit discovered a lump in her breast. They dealt with the problem swiftly starting with a visit to the local hospital in New Rochelle where the doctors performed a biopsy. It turned out to be malignant. Their next stop was Sloan Kettering in New York City where the head of oncology took Frank aside and said, "If you don't operate immediately, 18 months, that's all you have. Come back Monday for your surgery or never come back again."

Without delay Margit had her operation followed by chemotherapy. She lost her hair, then it grew back, gray. She became bloated. They continued with their lives, pretending everything was normal. The kids knew she was sick, but Frank and Margit downplayed how serious it was. They were hopeful it would all end in a good way.

Margit cooked favorite dinners and volunteered at the school library. She cheered at soccer games, the tall lady with the brightly colored scarves on her head, the one who never complained and never spoke about her illness. She was deteriorating, but kept herself together for David's bar mitzvah, baking pies and cakes for the celebration in their house.

"They pumped her up with chemotherapy; with poison that we hoped would find the right places to destroy while leaving the healthy cells alone," Frank said. "But there were no arrows or street signs to direct the chemicals."

It was trial and error. One set of formulas was used for three or four months. Then the doctors changed to another set. Frank and Margit became discouraged, so they switched hospitals. They tried Mt. Sinai. At least this time Margit liked her new doctor, Dr. Greenspan, though he chastised her for not coming to him first. For a short while, she was stabilized. She insisted on facing chemotherapy alone. After, she would walk from the treatment center to Frank's office, about a mile and a half, where they would go to lunch before she rode the train home.

"We believed she would recover. With renewed hope we took a break and visited Chezzi and his family in Israel."

Toward the end of the trip, while relaxing under an umbrella in the boiling heat at the Dead Sea, Frank stared at the scar above Margit's bathing suit. It seemed to sizzle and grow. In a panic, they flew home the next day to face the beginning of the end. She did not do well and had to go back to the hospital.

His sister-in-law knew someone in Arizona—a witch doctor or medicine woman. She worked with crystals and those sorts of things. Nobody knew exactly what she was. They never went there.

"Maybe we should have," Frank said. "Maybe I should have at least considered listening instead of being blinded solely by Western medicine."

They tried everything. They heard of a special drug that could be purchased in France, but not in the United States so Frank asked a friend who was visiting Paris to see a doctor who prescribed the medicine. His friend took the medicine to an acquaintance, a U.S. citizen working at a Swiss bank. He slipped it into one of their bank pouches to America. Frank and Margit waited for it to be delivered.

By this time it was August and Michael was starting his freshman year at Clemson University in South Carolina. David was 13 and away at soccer camp. Frank drove to the camp. He and David climbed to the top of a hill overlooking a meadow and the soccer field. Frank told David that his mother was in the hospital and was never going to come home again. They hugged and cried. Then they hugged and cried again and again and again.

"I thought it was the worst day of my life," Frank said. "But it got worse."

For the past year Frank had watched his wife endure pain. When she was home, he stayed up at night listening to her breathe. When she became weaker she went back into the hospital. At this point, there was nothing anyone could do to save her. Every day, for three weeks, Frank went to the hospital. He managed to get David to see his mother before she passed, but Michael was away at school.

"She was very sick," he said, "and I felt guilty admitting that I thought, *let her stop suffering already*."

Before she breathed her last breath she said, "Frank, I want you to get married quickly. Don't stay alone."

This was the furthest idea from Frank's mind, but it appeared to make her feel calm so he just listened while he held her hand. In August of 1981 Margit was 42. She died exactly 18 months from the day of the conversation with her first doctor. Frank was 47. Shortly after she passed, the medicine from Europe arrived.

Then Frank faced the next horror—how to tell his boys. With strong German upbringing, he pulled himself together. The night she died, Frank called one of his business friends, John Hollingsworth, in Greenville, South Carolina, who arranged to send one of his company's private planes to pick up Michael in a football field at Clemson University. They flew him to Charlotte, North Carolina, where he boarded a commercial flight home. He was in his father's arms by 10:00 a.m.

Frank's sister, her husband, Don, and their two boys, Josh and Barak, flew from Tennessee in time to see Margit before she passed away. After she passed, Margit's family flew in from California. Frank's cousins also were by his side. After everyone gathered in the funeral home, Frank walked his boys through the procedures without talking to anyone. They were the last to walk in and the first to walk out. The crowd was huge. Suppliers from Europe and clients and friends and family from Los Angeles joined local friends and relatives from Westchester.

"More people were there than were at our wedding," Frank said.

Children from school were seated together. Kevin Gilligan, David's friend who was only 13 years old, was the first person to bring Frank flowers. He had lost his father when he was 9.

"I know what it's like," he said.

This tall blond boy of Scottish ancestry became so close to David's father that he still calls Frank *abba*, just like Frank's sons.

At the cemetery Margit was buried near their baby son. Frank held David and Michael tightly as her body was lowered into the Earth.

"We were sobbing," he said. "I don't know how we were able to toss three shovelfuls of soil over the casket. I'm not sure it gave us the closure this Jewish custom is supposed to provide. We then threw red roses, Margit's favorite flower, into the grave. I think everyone was sobbing. That night David slept on my bed."

"Did you make a tear on your clothes?" I asked. "On the left side for a parent—the right side for a brother or sister, children and spouses? In my family when we mourn we don't wear leather shoes or jewelry and we sit on hard surfaces for seven days. Those are probably traditions from Russia that my family still embraces."

"No, I chose not to do any of that," he said.

Back at the house Diane and Irwin Friedman, two dear friends, came to comfort Frank. Edna Schenkel and Carol Matcovsky brought food to the house after the cemetery. They had worked with Frank at the synagogue when he had been President. Every night other friends carried in meals.

"My young nephew, Barak, helped cousin Laurel and her husband, Bill, cook a dinner," Frank said.

At seven o'clock the Rabbi came to gather ten men for the evening prayer and Kaddish, the prayer for the dead.

Frank's friends, Harvey and Tobey, drove every night from their home in New Jersey. Harvey pointed out two single women who also appeared every night until the *shiva*, the mourning period to honor the dead, was over. Perhaps they had mixed motives. They did not know what to say to make him feel better.

"It is hard to say or do the right thing in such a situation," Frank said. "It is hard for an outsider to know how you feel and react the right way. I never noticed the women but I tried to accept the niceties people were offering. Despite my grief, I appreciated the evening company and confusion that helped us get through the first week."

When *shiva* was up, everything stopped. Nobody showed up. Nobody called. For the outside world, it was over.

"For Michael, David and me," Frank said, "it was just beginning."

29: Mr. Mom

1982   Start of the Susan G. Komen for the Cure®
grassroots network dedicated to fight breast cancer.

After Margit passed away Frank moved his office from Manhattan to his house in Larchmont so he could be home for David after school. At the time it was not common for people to work from home, but he was sure his clients and suppliers would understand.

"As a commuter I figure I had logged 40 minutes each way, five days a week, 50 weeks a year for 15 years. I had lost 5,000 hours sitting on a train," Frank said. "I welcomed the idea of extra time."

First he had to remove a boulder that was in the middle of his basement. It was five feet high and six feet wide and took up most of the usable space. He tried to break it down with a five-horsepower pneumatic drill. No luck. He hired a professional road building company. They removed seven truckloads of granite. Seven massive truckloads! Finally, he was able to build three office rooms, a bathroom and a closet.

A friend suggested that Frank hire Marta, a housekeeper who was working for the friend, because

Frank needed help more than the friend did. Marta was wonderful. She came from Belize and cooked rice and beans with chicken and vegetables. David didn't like her meals because they were different from the pot roast and potatoes his mom had served. There were many other adjustments to be made. Almost every weekend Frank's mother, Hilda, and the housekeeper watched David while Frank traveled to South Carolina to be with Michael.

"I had been the kind of husband who didn't help around the house," Frank said. "I worked and traveled and the rest was always Margit's job, even buying my clothes."

He had never been to the supermarket. Suddenly he was shopping for food, doing the laundry, helping with homework. He was folding clothes, deciding menus, shoveling snow, moving cars, changing light bulbs and forever putting things in order. David, who would eventually become 6'1", was quickly growing out of his shoes and pants and Frank took him shopping at Benjamin's, the same store where Aunt Stella had bought him his first pair of corduroy slacks.

Frank wanted to do something special in memory of Margit. In 1943 a non-profit Children's Home had been established in Jerusalem to help Israel's most at-risk children recover from the Holocaust and war. It fulfilled the needs of 25 traumatized boys. These were the same children Chezzi, had welcomed upon their arrival in Palestine.

Frank and Margit were familiar with the home because in 1957, after Chezzi earned his Ph.D. in psychology and became a Board Certified Psychoanalyst, he became their director. Chezzi's philosophy of treatment without medical drugs made the school a leading facility in Israel and has served as a prototype for other groups. His work has earned him many honors and he is a speaker all over the world, including Germany.

Margit had been quite taken with this center and had been concerned that the boys had no place to go after they served a mandatory stint in the army. In his wife's honor, Frank started an extension for the older residents—a place they could return to after their tour in the military.

In Margit's name, Frank and his family provided rooms in a communal apartment along with psychiatric supervision to help the returning soldiers adjust to civilian life. Later, the Women's Division of B'nai B'rith in America partnered with them to provide additional funding. Today the home houses 86-100 boys and girls ages 7-18, with a one-to-one staff-to-child ratio.

"In my heart I wanted to tell Margit about the new residence," Frank said. "Sometimes, in the early evening, I'd say, 'Honey, let me tell you about my day.'"

"Margit never answered," Frank said looking down. "So I stopped."

30: Silence Says it All

1985 Ronald Reagan sworn in for his second term as President of the USA.

Mikhail Gorbachev becomes General Secretary of the Soviet Communist Party.

East Germany is freed, but citizens still suffer economic problems of having lived in a police state.

Throughout his adult years Frank had often asked his parents about life in their homeland. Their answers were brief, never enough, never much beyond the names and relationships of many relatives. He hoped for some insights in the early 1980s, when Hilda agreed to take a side trip to Crivitz, Germany, where her ancestors once lived.

Crivitz had been in the German Democratic Republic, the East German part of the country with its socialist poverty, secret police and repressive regulations. Frank hoped to learn about his heritage, to fill in some gaps for his boys as well as for himself.

On their way to a textile machine show in Milan they flew to Berlin then drove north for two hours on narrow, surprisingly well-paved roads. As they got closer to Crivitz they noticed fewer and fewer cars, another reminder they were in communist territory.

In town they stood behind a metal fence while Frank watched his mother stare at a bench on the side of the small brick train station. When your past smacks you hard in your face, how many minutes does it take to absorb the choices you've made? You can't go back, can't change anything. Perhaps it's easier when you know deep in your belly, below your conscious being, buried under 50 years of living, there really were no other options.

"It seems like the same bench I sat on close to 50 years ago," Hilda said. "Look up. You can see the same oversized clock mounted perpendicularly on the building. I'm sure passengers still count on it to determine the arrival of the next train, always on time, the German way. The only thing missing is my grandmother who used to meet me when I visited from Berlin," she said.

"We were quiet," Frank said. "I was searching hungrily for a glimpse of my ancestors. She was trying to forget the pain such memories brought."

Frank took a deep breath standing freely at the Crivitz train station—most likely at the same place where the small Jewish community of the town had been transported to work, then gassed in concentration camps. Perhaps this included Frank's great aunts and uncles and the complacent cousins who refused to believe the realities of the Third Reich and chose to stay. All were killed.

"The year you were born," Frank's mother said, "Nazi rallies, parades and marches celebrated a new era. Hitler was an excellent speaker, promising democracy, freedom and jobs for workers. It sounded wonderful, but we knew those improvements did not include us."

"Whenever I had asked my parents why they left Germany so early, my mother always repeated, 'I read *Mein Kampf*, Hitler's manifesto stating he would destroy the Jews. I didn't wait for him to kill us. I don't understand how so many people chose to ignore what was happening.'"

"Her answer was too simple for me," Frank said. I had to read history books to learn the truth."

"My grandfather had told me more stories than my mother ever did. The moment we drove along the lake in Crivitz I knew we had arrived," Frank said. "Fifty years later it looked just as he had described it when I was a kid in Bat Yam."

The cobblestone streets were bordered with small, attached brick or stone houses, each different with windows trimmed in dark brown or painted white wood, a vision that might have been lifted from an illustration in a Hansel and Gretel book.

No people were in the streets. Without any help, Hilda found the four-story brick house that had belonged to her ancestors. Thanks to the two top floors that had been added in 1917, it was the tallest building on the block, the Jacobson department store once owned by Hilda's family. There are family photos of him with his brothers and cousins dressed in suits and ironed shirts standing in front of the shop window.

The next owner was Alfred Jacobson, Hilda's uncle. On the day of Frank and Hilda's visit, the old family store still stood on the main street that had been renamed Parchimerstrasse. The apartment across the street reminded Hilda of her aunt who had enjoyed leaning on the windowsill watching life walk by below. A mound of coal used to heat the buildings long ago. A new black pile was stacked behind the Jacobson store just like Frank's grandfather had recalled. The big difference was the atmosphere.

Years ago employers were required to provide housing as well as jobs for their employees. By coincidence an old woman came out from the flat above. Hilda recognized her as Gerda Dumpelfeld whose mother had been a seamstress at the Jacobson shop. They had been friendly as children.

"I did not find out until years later that their serendipitous meeting was the start of a correspondence that lasted for many years," Frank said. "The letters my mother wrote were given to Fritz Rohde who included news about her and our family in the town's 750-year anniversary book."

Despite the quaint beauty of the area, I imagined the East German ambiance everywhere. Yellow, red and black East German flags were flying on many houses, including what had been my grandfather's home. The flags were the same tri-color horizontal bands as West Germany's flag except the East flags included a coat of arms in the center.

The old city seemed dead. There were few cars and fewer people. No buses were lined up at the bus station. People stayed indoors, behind closed curtains, perhaps not trusting each other, avoiding attention. It was still a communist country with powerful secret police.

While Hilda observed her surroundings, Frank smiled at the thought of being in the town of his ancestors, remembering his grandfather with much love. *Opi*'s stories were coming alive like photo albums shifting to video with sound and movement.

"I was thrilled to be where he had grown up, where he once strolled," Frank said.

As they were leaving, they passed the butcher shop where Hilda's great grandmother used to buy sausages. Mother became shy. She refused to make contact. Frank took over. He rang the bell, concerned about what to say when the owners opened the door.

"My hesitation wasn't necessary," he said. "The minute I explained who we were, the shocked family begged us to come in, to enjoy coffee and homemade cake and, most of all, tell them how we were able to survive."

There was one last item on Frank's nostalgia list— to see the Jewish cemetery Hilda had often visited with her grandfather.

"I felt connected," Frank said. "My bloodline started here. My great grandfather and my grandfather were born here."

"We would walk silently to the Jewish cemetery that was surrounded by a cement wall," mother said. "I used to put one of my small hands in my grandfather's hand and hold a flower in my other hand. Once there, grandfather would pull out his big iron key to unlock the iron gate. We would walk inside, still in silence, to place small stones and flowers on my grandmother's gravesite. A huge oak tree in the center of the cemetery had a big iron cross commemorating the Jewish soldiers who had given their lives for their fatherland in WWI."

Frank and Hilda wandered around not able to find the burial grounds. One woman stopped her car. "You must be visitors," she said in German. "Can I help you?" She led them to the place that used to be the Jewish cemetery before it was leveled, before a private home was erected over it, before the surrounding land became a soccer field where players sometimes tripped on gravestones protruding from the grass. Frank still had many questions.

Back in East Berlin they checked out the Berthold Levy Publishing Company, now an empty three-story building. Their final stop was the Handelshochschule, the university the Nazis had forced Hilda to quit. A security guard stopped them. Frank asked to talk to the head of the Department of Economics. While his mother reminisced about kissing her boyfriend under the stairs down the hall the Economics professor appeared. Again, Hilda turned quiet.

"My mother attended this university before WWII," Frank said. "She had to leave and never finished her studies. Now she would like to earn a Ph.D. in Economics," Frank said. "Can she complete your program by mail?"

The professor responded in very formal German. He ignored Hilda and spoke directly to Frank.

"My dear Mr. Levy, there is no way one can be educated by mail in a socialist country. Our system is much more complicated than your American capitalist system."

While mother stood by, he shook Frank's hand then dismissed them.

"I vowed that back in the USA we would locate a school that would accept mother as a student," Frank said, "in person or long distance."

In 1989, on her 80th birthday, Hilda graduated with a Ph.D. in Economics from Century University in Los Angeles. Her thesis was on International Trade between the United States and Czechoslovakia. Aside from three visits to school, classes and homework were exchanged by mail.

Did Hilda face down her past on that trip to Crivitz or was it when she completed her Ph.D.? How many other important milestones did she neglect to share?

"I'll never know," Frank said. "The one thing I remember most was her silence."

Herbert & Fred Levy united in America.

Hilda, Fred, Frank, Margit, Renee, Helga & Max in Beverly Hills, California.

Joshua, Ada, Don & Barak Olins.

Frank & Margit
June 21st, 1959.

Frank, Margit, David & Michael Levy.

Hilda with Grandma Marta
& Fred at their house in
The Bronx.

Laurel, Aunt Stella, Jeffrey, Beryl & Uncle Herbert
in Larchmont, New York.

Fred ready for Frank to take
him for a ride in San Luis
Obispo, California.

Frank & Chezzi with their wives and children in Jerusalem, 1976.
Back right: Miriam & Kurt.
(Chezzi's sister & brother-in-law).

Levy house in Larchmont, New York.

Frank, David & Michael Levy in Zermatt, Switzerland, 1984.

The clock at the Crivitz
Train Station, 1984

Hilda Levy in front of the
Berthold Levy Publishing Company
in Berlin, 1984.

The Front of the Jacobson Store in Crivitz, Germany, 1920.

Part III
Another New Beginning
1982-2008

31: Moving On

*1983   The Brundtland Commission, also known as the
       World Commission on Environment and
       Development, is established by the United Nations to
       encourage countries to pursue sustainable
       development together.*

For two years after Margit died, it appeared that Frank was
doing well. He worked, coached soccer, cared for David
and Michael. In reality, he was stuck. Starting again was
harder than adapting to a new country.

"Margit's clothes were still in the closet," he said.
"I greeted her smiling photo every morning near my bed. I
couldn't find a way to jump over my shadow, to move
forward."

Frank had lived in a couples' world for 21 years. To
think about entering the unmarried arena at age 50 was
frightening. Staying alone seemed worse, but he had no
idea how to meet single women.

"How would I incorporate a new relationship with
my children the second time around? What should I wear?
Where should I take a date?"

A friend in Larchmont, a divorced man who was a psychiatrist, invited Frank to join him at a party in Connecticut. Wall-to-wall people filled the private home. As soon as Frank and his friend walked in, two women chatting on a couch hurried toward them.

"I don't remember what they looked like," Frank said. "I was in shock trying to decide what to say. I kept asking myself, *What am I doing here?*"

One woman told him, "Mister, you sure aren't ready to be dating."

Since he never talked about his loss, Frank had no idea what he had said to make her think that way, though she did point out he was still wearing his wedding band. It took him another year to remove the ring and start his quest.

First he found all the scraps of paper with names and phone numbers friends had given him—women they were sure would be perfect matches. After he met a few, he began to wonder if his friends knew him at all and why they thought he would like any of them. Next he made a list of Margit's single friends. They had so much in common, Frank thought that might be the way to go. None of them were right.

David said, "Dad, why don't you find a Rockette?"

Frank didn't tell him that kind of woman scared him.

Some of his married men friends thought he had a great opportunity. They made silly sex jokes and seemed jealous that he had a green light to pick up anyone he found attractive.

"They imagined I was in for some good times and interesting escapades and could hardly wait to hear all the details," he said. "I had no such illusions."

One early experience sums up the desperation of many of the single people in New York City. It was in such an old rickety building in Greenwich Village that the *yekke* in him decided he didn't like the woman before they met. She answered the door holding a glass of champagne. As he stepped over some clutter to get into her small, dark studio apartment, she leaned back on the couch that took up most of the room, bared her tummy then poured the champagne onto her skin.

"I felt so sorry for this frustrated person behaving inappropriately with a stranger," Frank said. "I turned around and left. My blind dates were disappointing. Maybe I needed to connect with someone who had a similar background to mine—someone of German or Israeli descent."

Frank wrote a letter to a well-known Jewish center in Frankfurt, Germany, explaining he was a widower, a mechanical engineer living in Westchester County with two sons and an international career, looking for a wife. Nobody at the Jewish Center answered. Instead, he received numerous letters and photographs from all kinds of women.

Somebody must have published his inquiry in the personal ad section of a local German newspaper. Many of the responses were from Eastern European women looking for a man in America, eager to be sponsored to come to the United States. They could hardly write in German. Their English was worse. He never contacted them.

The one exception was an Israeli immigrant from Bukara, Uzbekistan. He had to look at a map to see where she was from. On his next trip to Tel Aviv Frank called her. She was eager to meet because she wanted an escort for her daughter's wedding party—a three-day affair.

"We drove to deliver invitations and for two hours she did not stop talking," Frank said. "I envisioned being together for days, with a huge food festival and belly dancing and lots of people who spoke unfamiliar languages. I wouldn't know anybody. I didn't even know this lady. Although it would have been interesting to see such a celebration, it was totally overwhelming, so I passed."

In Israel, Frank met a local woman who joined him on a short business trip to Europe. Nothing serious was discussed, yet one day in Larchmont the doorbell rang and there she stood with a suitcase hoping to move in. He was afraid to let her come into the house, so he sent her to a friend.

He was discouraged yet so anxious to connect he made three coffee dates in one night. He called it smart dating. Have some coffee, conduct a quick interview and decide whether there was a future or not. Most were not. One night he forgot the name of his second date of the evening. Was it Judy, Joan or Carol? He couldn't remember, so he called David to look in his calendar and tell him whom he was meeting. David thought it was very funny and once again said, "Dad, try for a Rockette.'"

By now Frank had been dating for a few years and had forged some temporary relationships. Many of these single women lived in Manhattan on East 86th Street.

"I don't know why these tall buildings were full of potential mates," Frank said.

One girl ate only French food—not his taste. Another only played tennis. He hadn't yet learned. This one was very angry, especially with her ex. That one was weepy. Children sometimes became an issue. Someone didn't want him. He didn't want the next one.

"So much activity," Frank said, "but still I was alone."

Meanwhile, he was coaching his son's soccer games in Larchmont. One Saturday he saw me, the mother of one of David's best friends, my son, Michael M. My Michael sometimes ate dinner at Frank's house and David ate at mine.

"Michael and I had a wonderful rapport," Frank said. "That day you were standing alone across the field. I had noticed you before, but you always kept your distance. When you weren't there, your ex-husband came to the games and we chatted. He was very friendly."

Frank also had seen me at the train station carrying *The New York Times* when I commuted to work. Once or twice he tried to say hello or good morning.

"I was just being cordial to Michael's mother," Frank said. "But you always turned around and walked away in silence. You were rude."

"I noticed your wedding band," I said. "It wouldn't have been the first time a married man tried to pick me up and I have standards."

At the same time I had been asking my Michael to introduce me to David's father. I liked the fact that Frank had set up his office at home to be near his son when he came home from school.

"When I slighted you," I said, "I had no idea you were my Michael's soccer coach."

A few years later, during the 1988 Christmas break, Frank took his sons and some of their friends to his ski house. One of those boys was my Michael. I was one of three single women visiting my friends, Linda and Neil Goldstein, in the area. The group pushed me to ask Michael if we could come by to say hello, but I resisted. Then, for the first time in my life, my car broke down. Fate. I arranged to have the car fixed and for Michael to drive it home at the end of the week.

My friends volunteered to drive me home but only if we stopped at Frank's house along the way. I had been trying to meet him for years and they insisted this was the day. I tried on all three sweaters I had brought for the weekend and everyone voted which one I should wear— just like in junior high school. I was excited and optimistic.

We called Michael to let him know we would be there soon.

Frank gave my Michael $20 to buy a cake or whatever his mother (me) would like to munch on with a cup of coffee. Frank knew I wasn't friendly, so he paid little attention to the situation.

Just before Neil pulled up the long unpaved driveway in the woods, it started to snow. I rang the bell. Frank opened the door. I slipped on some ice and fell into him. Shocked, I looked up and said, "Oh my God, I know you. I know you from the train."

"Yes," Frank said and that was the last communication we shared the entire evening.

My Michael is extremely social and well mannered. He tried to help me.

"Say something," he whispered in my ear. "Say anything." I stayed quiet.

Michael tried again. "Talk about the chicken I'm cooking." Silence. "It's snowing. Talk about the weather," he said.

I kept my mouth closed and my head down.

Years later Frank said, "I was glad your friends were talkative."

The following August, after David and both of my boys left for college, Frank walked past the local Citibank on his way to take a neighbor's son to lunch to celebrate his new junior driver's license. At that moment, I came out of the bank. Fate again. I was dressed in a tennis outfit, all legs, balancing dry cleaning with two large grocery bags that obstructed my view. Smack, I bumped into him. In the excitement of the moment I dropped everything. Oranges rolled down the street in one direction, eggs splattered in another. This time I knew it was Frank and, though flustered, I asked about his boys.

"I was surprised you were friendly," Frank said. "A real chatterbox."

Frank called me that night and left a monotone message in his Henry Kissinger accent.

"Hello, this is Frank Levy. I am David's father and I have been single for eight years and you have been single for 13 years and I thought we could get together and explore the possibilities."

It wasn't the smoothest opening, but I was tired of dating players who wore gold chains around their necks and were afraid of commitment.

"It was smooth enough," Frank said. "You fell for it."

I thought about the advertising executive who had visited during a weekend when my boys were with their dad. I told my date he could eat anything in the refrigerator except the Entenmann's cake because my son had bought it with his allowance. The man immediately cut himself a slice and left $.50 on the box. I never saw him again.

I thought about the Harvard businessman I had been engaged to a number of years before I met Frank, the one who wouldn't get off the phone to help me carry groceries and ended our relationship two weeks before our scheduled wedding.

These men had much in common: *GQ* style players from Ivy League colleges who could twirl me around the dance floor. Perhaps my priorities needed to be tweaked. It would be refreshing to go out with someone who was nice for a change, someone I could trust, so I called back late that night.

"I asked her out for coffee," Frank said. "When she accepted, I felt brave so I added dessert."

"Frank, we already met," I said on the phone. "We know each other's kids. Let's be really wild and go for dinner."

"I knew right then I was in trouble," he said. "Big trouble."

I was the one in trouble. I thought I was hot stuff. At the end of that dinner Frank walked me to the front of my apartment building. I closed my eyes, lifted my face and waited for a goodnight peck. All I felt was a breeze. When I heard him laugh and say good night, I realized I wasn't in as much control as I had imagined.

"By our third date I was hooked," Frank said. "I knew you were athletic and liked to jog, so I invited you for breakfast and a run to the Long Island Sound, about a mile and a half from my house. I put on an old pair of navy and green knit short shorts and matching short-sleeved shirt my housekeeper had ironed. I had never jogged, but wanted to make a good impression so I picked out a brown paisley silk ascot from my tie rack and wrapped it around my neck. I thought I looked very dapper."

I never said a word about his outfit. We also never went jogging. We lingered over breakfast and, totally out of character, Frank told me he thought we would get married. I thought so, too. It took us 18 months to complete that thought.

"I had imagined I needed someone with the same background," Frank said. "I didn't realize I had changed since my first marriage. I had become far more Americanized. Even my accent was lighter, less identifiable. Having sons the same age, living in the same community and living by the same family values became more important commonalities than speaking German or Hebrew or skiing. I had searched around the world but connected with the girl around the corner."

"There are songs about that," I said.

"If you say so," he said. "It's good that we are different. We both read the same *New York Times* but you gravitate to the *Arts and Leisure* section while I follow the influence of world events on our lives. It's enlightening to share details."

"Matching" and "presentation" are words I added to Frank's vocabulary along with a new red tie, longer short shorts and small-rimmed glasses. Because my career required me to attend lots of events I took Frank to publicity receptions and advertising award-show galas. He introduced me to textile machinery at international trade shows in Milan, Hamburg and Paris. I let him win at tennis, six to four, until he figured out a strategy and beat me on his own. All we had to do was get used to having two Michaels as well as a David and a Joel.

"She loves to cook for family gatherings," Frank said, "and let's not forget she's a really great dancer. I had found my Rockette."

32: A Broken Promise

1989   Fall of communism. Berlin Wall comes down.

June 4: Tiananmen Square massacre in Beijing against the government of The Peoples' Republic of China.

The non-violent Velvet Revolution ends communism in Czechoslovakia. Writer and poet Vaclav Havel becomes president of Czechoslovakia.

One Saturday Frank asked me to meet him at his synagogue though neither of us was religious. I liked being independent. Frank was far more involved in the community and enjoyed the togetherness the synagogue provided. He followed Jewish traditions but since his boys had left for college, he only went to services a few times a year. Perhaps he was trying to bridge his old life with the new when he asked me to join him.

"Margit and I had been part of a tight-knit group," Frank said, "After Margit died only some of the women embraced my new girlfriends. I hoped they would accept Marilyn."

"Given my religious diffidence, Frank was surprised I agreed to accompany him there. I was glad such a small thing, or at least a small amount of my time, could make him happy. Frank gave me the keys to his house and car and he walked to the synagogue. Our plan was for me to complete some errands in town then drive to temple in time for the rabbi's weekly sermon.

On his way to *shul* Frank stopped at Tony the tailor who had emigrated from Prato in the Tuscany region of Italy. They talked about the new Starbuck's, many young families moving into Larchmont, the cost of well-made Italian clothing. The two men shared an appreciation for fine fabrics. They both were naturalized American citizens with accents. They understood each other.

"I lost track of time," Frank said. "The moment I reached the temple, services were almost over and you weren't there. I was so disappointed."

When two people don't know each other well, it's easy to jump to negative conclusions, which is exactly what he did. He tried hard not to be disillusioned and decided to go forward with new experiences and to develop new memories.

"I just couldn't stop questioning whether or not I could trust you," he said. "I hoped you had a good reason for breaking your promise to meet me."

I did have a good reason. About two minutes after I opened the door to Frank's house, the alarm went off. Another minute later, the phone rang. The alarm company wanted to know the secret code. I had no clue, not even a guess. Immediately after I hung up, two cops came into the house and told me to stand right where I was.

The female police officer stayed with me while her partner poked into the attic and the basement office. The male cop checked the new kitchen with the black granite counter and investigated all four bathrooms. He looked behind the baby grand piano and the two couches in the living room. Then he started on all the closets. The search for an accomplice took less than ten uncomfortable minutes.

During this time the alarm kept screaming while the lights on top of the police car flashed outside. Some neighbors came out of their homes to see what was happening. I wasn't frightened because I hadn't done anything wrong and I lived in an apartment just a few blocks away.

"I'm Frank's girlfriend," I explained. "I live near here. Look at my driver's license. It's okay that I'm in the house."

"Look, lady, we don't mean to be difficult, but just because you live in Larchmont doesn't mean you belong here. We need to speak to Mr. Levy. Do you know where he is?"

"That's easy," I said. "He went to synagogue this morning and I promised to join him to hear the rabbi's sermon. He's at the conservative temple on the corner of Chatsworth and Boston Post Road."

"Okay, let's go," said the gentleman officer as he ushered me into the back seat of the police car. The burglar alarm was still piercing the stillness of the community and the police lights were still flashing as we drove off.

Along the way I spotted a woman walking to synagogue. She had been a good friend of Frank's first wife. I shouted to her, ecstatic that I had found someone who could identify me. The woman peered at me sitting in the back seat of the flashing cop car.

"Humph," she said. "It figures." Then she continued her walk to *shul*.

The cops stopped in front of the temple and escorted me, one on each arm, up the stairs.

"Please," I said to the officer on my right. "Let me go in alone. I won't run away. Let me go in by myself and I'll bring Frank out."

The cops stopped inside the vestibule between the front door and the sanctuary and let me proceed on my own. Once inside, I could see there were very few people in attendance. Frank was not there.

I admit that I did think about sneaking out the back door, but I had no idea where it was. The two officers escorted me back into their patrol car and drove me to Frank's house. By then the alarm had stopped and the police had checked my background. They let me go since I didn't have a record. I was left wondering what happened to Frank.

We met up later and Frank told me what his father often had told him in Bat Yam: "If the end is well, all is well."

33: Berlin, Prague and Zurich

*1987   June 12: U.S. President Ronald Reagan challenges
Mikhail Gorbachev, General Secretary of the Soviet
Union, to tear down the Berlin Wall as a symbol of
the increasing freedom of the Eastern bloc.*

*1989   November 17: The Velvet Revolution in Prague
frees Czechoslovakia.*

Three months after we started dating, a week after the
demise of the Berlin Wall, Frank took me on our first big
excursion to Berlin, Prague and Zurich.

"I wanted you to understand the relationship
between politics and the day-to-day existence of all
citizens, including those who might not pay attention to
current events," Frank said. "And I wanted you to
understand my life."

The trip was in November 1989, just before the
non-violent Velvet Revolution that changed
Czechoslovakia from Stalinism to a democracy. By the
time we arrived in Berlin much of the Wall had been
chiseled off for souvenirs. No fragments were left on the
ground. At Checkpoint Charlie in the Friedrichstrasse

neighborhood, Frank hired a taxi driver to bring us to the city's less populated Eastern section.

Despite a torrential downpour we stepped out of the car to snap photos of original murals painted on the cement—visual stories the East Germans had created about freedom. Portions of the Wall were strewn around the area. We gathered up enough for friends, relatives and ourselves. I slipped some smaller pieces into the pockets of my black leather jacket. Frank carried the larger chunks.

We asked the driver to take us to hear local musicians—jazz or folk or rock. My dad had worked his way through school playing saxophone in a band. In college I had minored in piano. I was anxious to hear how the Germans expressed their new freedom through music.

The driver dropped us at an old communist meeting place that had recently been turned into a coffee house. It was filled with amps and lights and musical groups taking turns on a makeshift stage. The audience was comprised of young people who seemed to be at least six and a half feet tall.

We looked out of place with our Western clothes, our advanced age and average height. Frank was still holding the largest of our cement pieces. The place was noisy and smoky. We lasted ten minutes then returned to our hotel to pack for the next segment of our vacation.

In Prague, Frank introduced me to Al Marek and his wife, Mary, who joined us in a restaurant decorated with animal heads on the wall. Though I was told it was a popular place, we were the only diners.

"You have to understand," Frank said, "this was still an Eastern Bloc country. People had little money to go out."

Leaving the city to go to Zurich the lines at the airport snaked around more than twice. The wait to check our baggage was long. Frank became nervous about missing the plane, a Russian military aircraft that had been altered to accommodate passengers.

As we inched ahead with the crowd, we approached the next checkpoint. I couldn't find my passport. Without my documents I would not be allowed to leave. But Frank had an important meeting in Switzerland. If he missed the plane, he would miss that appointment. It wasn't the German way not to show up and he couldn't call because this was before cell phones.

"I'll go ahead," he said as a joke. Or maybe he meant it. "You'll figure this out and meet me in Zurich."

There was a sinister feel to the country. I didn't speak Czech. I was stuck and my new boyfriend was about to abandon me. I started to cry. What else could I do? The moment I shed tears, a guard approached and asked me my name in English. He smiled and held up my passport. I had left it at the check-in counter and he was watching the crowd, searching for anyone who looked Western, waiting for someone to ask for the passport.

Was Frank teasing when he told me he would leave me in Prague? I'll never know for sure. I clung to the new phrase he had spouted: "If the end is well, all is well." Still, I couldn't stop questioning whether or not I could trust him.

Shortly after we returned to the States, I read the headlines in the newspapers. Without violence, without shooting, the people of Czechoslovakia had ended communism and converted to a parliamentary republic. Barbed wire was removed from the borders with West Germany and Austria. Vaclav Havel was elected the first President.

"It was unimaginable!" Frank said. "Maybe it's a sign that it is possible for opposing groups in the Middle East to solve their differences without guns."

We soon heard that Mr. Holub, the man who had given Frank the clown art, had been in charge of building the watchtowers where soldiers prevented Czech people from escaping to the West. He kept miniature models of the towers on a shelf behind his desk so everyone knew his involvement. After the uprising, the towers were torn down. Communists who once ruled became the enemy and Holub became frightened. Rather than face any repercussions, he committed suicide.

By the summer of 1990 the atmosphere in Czechoslovakia was more open. Frank arranged for my son, Joel, and his college friend to teach English to the workers at The Cotton Research Institute outside of Prague. Joel was able to appreciate the economic challenges facing Czech citizens who lost their economic security and didn't know how to compete in a free market. At the same time he saw the onset of the exciting transformation brought about with capitalism—open cafes, shops filled with products, castles sparkling with lights, rebuilt hotels and varied architecture as the city moved toward becoming a mini Paris.

Private entrepreneurs were able to take over the Investa businesses. The Czechs traveled to America, to South Carolina to open their own sales office. They gave Frank the option to purchase 50% of their company. He declined. Investa kept him as their agent on a commission basis, but he was no longer needed. What was exciting for Joel was catastrophic for Frank.

"I don't know how many Americans paid attention to this important political development," Frank said. "For me it was the end of a good portion of my business. It was time to reinvent myself again."

As Frank's son, David, once said to me, "My father is a giant who builds and accomplishes because he understands, adapts and innovates."

Frank had always wanted to save the land. He shifted his focus to recycling textile waste, this time selling machines made in Italy.

34: One Wedding, Two Honeymoons

1991 April 21: Frank and Marilyn marry.

December: The Cold War ends.
Mikhail Gorbachev, President of the Soviet Union,
resigns.

Dissolution of the Soviet Union. Boris Yeltsin
becomes President of Russia.

When David graduated from high school in 1986, Frank carried his living room furniture to the garage and set up a black-tie dinner party for about a dozen of his son's friends and their dates. My Michael was among them.

"I never understood why none of the mothers offered to help," Frank said, "but I was happy to host this celebration before the limos arrived to take the couples to their senior prom."

Four years later, during the 1990 Thanksgiving weekend, many of the same high school friends came by to say hello to Frank. I was sitting in the living room near the front door. David and my Michael were in the den. As each boy entered the house he registered surprise to see Michael's mother with Frank. We could hear them whispering.

Michael Levy and my younger son, Joel, are talkers, but my Michael and David seem to communicate with eye contact. Whole paragraphs are conveyed with a glance, a nod or a shrug. It's as If they have their own language. Frank remembers Michael M. saying to David: "Looks like we're going to be stepbrothers."

"Cool," was David's reply.

"Yeah, cool," Michael M. added, which seemed to cover the situation.

For my 48th birthday Frank planned a different surprise. Joel, who was studying at Colgate University, was spending his junior semester in Geneva, Switzerland. Frank arranged for him and his date to meet us at the Jungfrau mountain region near Geneva. When they arrived, the hotel Frank had selected was boarded up. It was before cell phones, so there was no way to communicate. Frank and I searched many other hotels, but couldn't find them. We gave up and picked a place at random near the train station. By coincidence it was the same place Joel had selected.

When Joel and his date boarded the train to return to school, he held the Swiss chocolates Frank had bought for them and said, "Mom, we decided, if you don't marry him, we will."

On another occasion Frank shifted his investments to Citibank. In appreciation for his business, the bank gave him two tickets, a hotel room and free airfare to a Super Bowl game. David and Joel hardly knew each other. Both were avid football fans.

"Football never interested me," Frank said, "so I sent them to the game together."

Despite these generous gestures, merging families is never easy.

"When I told my mother we were engaged," Frank said, "her response was, 'Why would you want to do that?'"

Hilda was not a fan of any woman who couldn't speak German. She always asked me where I was from. I told her Larchmont, but she was more interested in where my ancestors had come from so I told her I was from *Fiddler on the Roof*. She didn't laugh. She insisted that "Gottlieb" means love of God in German and therefore I must be German, even if I thought I was of Russian descent and my grandparents had spoken Russian. I still can hear her asking, in her thick German accent, "Are you SURE you aren't German?"

Later we shared the good news with my mom. She told Frank, "Thank God you're taking her off my hands." I am an independent businesswoman who raised two sons with my ex husband in a joint custody arrangement. I didn't need my mother's help, but moms and dads carry their own sense of everlasting responsibility.

Parents are only part of the blending equation. The second time around kids count more. Frank being Frank invited both my boys to spend a weekend with us in his ski house.

When I called my Michael, there was a long pause before he said, "My skis are in Frank's house. I have been skiing there for years. Mom, you're the new one."

"Right," I said realizing how lucky we were. I smiled when he added, "And by the way, he will surprise you with a hot tub. Why don't you surprise him with a bathing suit?"

Getting married wasn't so easy. Though I had a civil divorce, Frank's rabbi refused to marry us unless I could show him a Get, a Jewish divorce document presented by a husband to his wife. I called my ex and he joked away the tension. Once I got a Get Frank's sister took all of Margit's clothes from the closet to make room for my things.

Last on the list was a matter of taste: my pink floral couch versus his Danish modern furniture, my dishes or his, painted white walls or dark wood panels? Shag carpet with orange accents or oriental area rugs? It took a decorator skilled in arbitration, a man named Dan Kizer, to help us complete this task.

Three months later Frank and I stood before the rabbi as he read the *ketubah*, our religious wedding contract printed on beautiful parchment paper. While I tried to memorize the details of this extraordinary moment, the rabbi asked me to sign my name in Hebrew.

"I don't know it in Hebrew," I said over the sound of rain pouring on the roof.

"You have to sign your name in Hebrew," he repeated ever so softly, making it difficult for our two witnesses to understand the dilemma.

We were in a small room near the banquet hall at the Beach Point Club on the Long Island Sound in Mamaroneck. Uncle Herbert was a member and he had enabled us to arrange our Sunday breakfast wedding celebration there in grand style, far grander than I had envisioned for a second wedding in the middle of my life.

Months before I had wanted the blending of our two families to be private—just our grown sons, our moms, my brother, Frank's sister and their respective families. But Frank had insisted we add his uncle. At the time I didn't understand why Herbert was so important. All I realized was that we also had to embrace Herbert's grown children and their families.

"Those are cousins," I said. "If you invite your cousins, I must ask my cousins and since it is no longer just the immediate family we might as well invite our friends."

Might as well is a dangerous phrase. By the time we mailed the invitations we were up to 150 people—a multigenerational assortment of well-wishers—local cousins, cousins from California, our friends and their kids and our neighbors. We encouraged our sons to invite their friends so they could feel super comfortable. The "yes" list included Frank's customers from the Southern and Western parts of the country as well as a supplier from Italy.

On my side were senior executives from the ad agency where I worked as a publicist in Manhattan—writers, producers, media buyers and account supervisors in navy blue suits. And there was a smattering of reporters who had become friends.

Everyone gathered around the *chuppah*, the canopy symbolizing the home Frank and I would build together. Each of our boys supported one of the four poles that held up the silk white cloth, the prayer shawl that had been worn by Frank's father. All we had to do was emerge from the side room.

"I don't know how to write my name in Hebrew," I said again, buttoning and unbuttoning my pale blue silk blazer that matched my sleeveless silk sheath. Something blue. My pearls had once belonged to my grandmother. Something old. I had borrowed something, I don't remember what, and my cream high heels were new. I was ready for the ceremony if only we could get past this signing business.

I turned toward Frank who grabbed my hand that clutched a pen. He moved my wrist across the *ketubah* and scribbled letters I didn't recognize: my name in Hebrew.

We married with joy, knowing that Uncle Herbert, who had passed away 25 days earlier, had given us his blessing.

We honeymooned in the Caribbean, in Anguilla. Since our kids were too old for all of us to live together, we also decided to create some shared memories. That summer we rented an apartment in Aspen, Colorado during the classical music festival. We took the boys and David's girlfriend, Carolyn, whom he had met at Brandeis University. They hoped to marry when she completed her residency at New York's Mt. Sinai Hospital and before her Fellowship in Pediatric Oncology at Memorial Sloan Kettering in New York City. In Aspen we hiked, rode bikes, fished, watched a rodeo, attended a crafts fair and enjoyed a river rafting experience.

During the vacation, David and Carolyn roller bladed to Maroon Bells, a lake where he proposed. The shared memories had begun.

35: The Textile Industry Moves To China

1903   A German-British joint venture founded the
Germania Brewery in Quingdao, China, that later
became known as the Tsingtao Brewery.

1984   Quingdao, a strategic seaport in the eastern section
of China, was granted an open-door policy to
foreign trade and investment.

1992   Quingdao became a free-trade zone.

We stood and toasted Frank, the Americans on one side of
the mahogany table and the Chinese on the other. The
boardroom in Quingdao, pronounced Ching Dow, was as
elegant as any conference room in a large ad agency in
Manhattan—deep black leather swivel chairs, long polished
table, bottles of water with empty drinking glasses, pads of
paper and pens. The meeting in the Eastern Shandong
Province was to discuss the possibility of Frank's clients
purchasing machinery made in China.

All aspects of the American textile industry was
disappearing, eroding and shifting to China way before our
trip in 2005. Frank felt it was time to see what the

competition offered. Such an excursion should have been tackled years ago. Attending an international textile machinery show in Shanghai was the perfect catalyst to make it happen.

A few days earlier Paul and Shirley Turner from Beverly Hills and Marty Zeldin and his girlfriend from Philadelphia met us in Shanghai to attend the show. Shirley and I had developed a strong friendship over the years, traveling with our husbands to Italy and then most countries in Europe. It was our first time in Asia and we were dazzled by the mixture of Chinese, European and ultra modern architecture in Shanghai.

The newer mega structures ranged from slim curved glass buildings to the Oriental Pearl TV Tower. One hotel boasted 88 stories with the longest laundry shoot. Another claimed to have the largest glass stairway. At night the vibrant modern buildings, bathed in lights, were more magical than anything I had seen in New York, Chicago or even Disney World. There were more new cars than bicycles and the hotels were inexpensive yet beyond five-star luxurious. We even had our own private butler.

The machine show was so enormous it took us an hour to walk from the entrance to the textile carding machines. Along the way we passed machines for weaving, knitting, printing on fabric, cutting, sewing and embroidering bold colorful patterns onto fabrics. People of every skin color, ethnic group, country and language were represented. Everyone was dressed in western business attire and seemed to move with a sense of purpose. The three-story high ceilings swallowed most noise and florescent lighting kept the areas bathed in midday brightness. Escalators carried a constant stream of people from one exhibit to restaurants and other exhibits.

As we hiked from building to building Frank was animated, excited to talk about machines and problems his engineering skills could solve, always moving forward, creating something to make business and the environment better. It was a thread throughout his life, part of his sense of self. In contrast, my eyes glazed over, though I tried to stay focused on our map that showed where to find each exhibit.

"Without a carding machine you can't make yarn," Frank said. "Today it's a major financial investment for a mill owner to buy a card because these machines are expensive and have a long life. The decision of which one to purchase is critical."

"Aren't they all the same?" I asked.

"No, definitely not. You have to understand, it's not so simple. There are cards for the cotton industry and others for the woolen industry. They each use different technology to force entangled fibers to line up in a parallel so they can be fed into spinning machines that make yarn. It's like combing tangled hair.

"Hollingsworth in Greenville, South Carolina, used to make all the wires for carding machines in America, South America and Europe. At the show it seemed to me there were very few electronic controls for these machines. Everything was done by hand. In China it seemed to me as if nothing was automated like the new machines we see in Europe and the States."

Frank and I had started this trip in Prato, Italy where we bought some Limoncello—lemon liqueur—and a bottle of red wine from the Carmignano region to share before our clients went home. We carried the bottles with us when we flew from Shanghai to Qingdao. The city has beautiful beaches along the Yellow Sea and lots of good beer, a legacy from the Germans who once occupied the city from 1898 to 1914. In Qingdao our group was scheduled to observe factories that were manufacturing carding machines.

"Cotton cards are 40 inches wide. Nonwoven cards are much bigger, 100-120 inches wide," Frank said. "The Chinese were building two nonwoven cards and up to 70 cotton cards per day."

To accomplish this goal they had their own foundry with 70 buildings and about 7,000 employees. It was a labor-intensive endeavor. In the 1800s, cards were made out of wood and were slow. Later, the sidewalls were cast iron. They were so heavy manufacturers needed a crane to assemble them.

Today cards are made out of steel with some of the cylinders 60-80 inches in diameter and 100 inches long. The kind of card one chooses depends upon what kind of fibers one wants to process. They can be wool, recycled wool, blended wool, cotton, blended cotton and other variations.

"The demand for cards is so high I think the Chinese can't produce enough cards for their own citizens and also export them to other countries," Frank said. "If every Chinese person needed one t-shirt, there would not be an adequate number of carding machines to produce enough shirts for that market."

In Qingdao, while the other women went shopping, I opted to join Frank in the factories to see the machines. It was quiet. There were no people—except for our escorts. Nothing was running. Maybe it was a lunch break. Maybe the company lacked electricity and ran at 10-20% efficiency.

"I think American plants usually run at 98% efficiency," Frank said. "But there are over a billion people in China who need jobs compared to an estimated 300 million people in America. With more workers available, wages are lower and Chinese goods are sold to the USA at a lower price."

After our tour we were brought to the conference room. Paul asked, "What happens if the electrical panel needs to be replaced?"

The head of the Chinese group stood, tapped his water glass and said, "A toast to Mr. Paul Turner."

We all rose and lifted our water to toast Paul.

Then Marty asked, "What happens if we need new lags or an engineer to help us?"

The head of the Chinese group stood again, tapped his water glass and said, "A toast to Mr. Marty Zeldin."

We all rose and lifted our water to toast Marty.

The meeting proceeded with lots of questions and lots of toasts until we were escorted to a different building. Rows of fish tanks were set into every wall in the lobby, much like a beautiful modern aquarium. Each species floated in its own tank. Upstairs in a private banquet room I realized those fish were the menu. When it was my turn to order, I became a vegetarian.

I watched the Lazy Susan circle lobster toward Paul and Frank. It looked raw. While I ate broccoli and asparagus, I saw them dip their chopsticks into the lobster. As they filled their mouths with the delicacy, I swear the lobster's antennae moved.

Our last stop was Beijing for a mini vacation, a tour of Tiananmen Square, the Forbidden Palace as well as a section of the Great Wall. Before departing we invited our friends to our room to share our Limoncello and Italian red wine. We opened the box and found two bottles of cheap Chinese wine. The Chinese inspectors at the border had orchestrated an exchange right in front of Frank.

"I watched the examiners pack the bottles into a Styrofoam container. Their hands were so fast," Frank said, "I never realized they made a switch."

Frank and his clients decided not to work with China, not to buy machinery in Qingdao. It might have been cheaper, but they were worried about follow up service and the quality of the machines.

"In comparison to the Chinese equipment," Frank said, "my partner, Sergio, builds machines that are somewhat of an art. Of course he guarantees his machines and services them when needed."

Obviously other American manufacturers have had different experiences with the Chinese and are able to take advantage of the cheap labor and better exchange rates between the dollar and the local Yuan. But machines are not consumer goods. Since each line must be prepared uniquely for the buyer, Frank and Sergio are better able to service American.

"If all manufacturing, especially of consumer goods, stays in underdeveloped countries, it takes jobs away from our people," Frank said. "It creates huge unemployment in America. At the same time, the world is flat and competition is global. I don't know how to solve this problem."

36: Connecting The Dots

*1992 The Israeli Embassy in Buenos Aires is bombed.
Islamic Jihad Organization claims responsibility.*

How do you unite a lengthy past with a second family? Sisters, brothers, nieces and nephews are easy. But Frank wanted more, so we joined my ex, his wife and their daughter for Thanksgiving feasts and Father's Day celebrations. Frank brought me to California to develop a relationship with Margit's brother, Frank, and Frank's sister, Renee. He introduced me to Sergio and his family outside Florence, Italy and then walked me through the factory to observe textile-recycling machinery. Later, in America, he took me to his clients' plants. It wasn't enough. He yearned for me to see where he was from, to appreciate the meanings behind his accent and to understand his thoughts.

That's what Frank hoped to accomplish when he took me on my first trip to Israel the year after we were married. The timing was perfect. Chezzi was celebrating his 60th birthday with a party in a restaurant at Mishkenot Sha'ananim, across from Mt. Zion outside the walls of the

Old City of Jerusalem. It was a chance for us to meet and for Frank to catch up with Chezzi and his family.

Joel had just graduated from college and he, too, had never been to the Middle East, so as a graduation gift, Frank took him along. I gave Joel some cash with a caveat. He had to use the money to buy a piece of art to remember the trip.

Gidi, Frank's distant cousin from Gan Shmuel, met us at the Tel Aviv Airport in a battered blue pickup truck. Gidi and Frank sat in front. I climbed into the open back with the luggage. From there we swung by a hotel to collect Joel and his then-girlfriend who both joined me in back for the 50-minute drive north to the kibbutz.

We ate meals in the communal dining room, enjoying crisp cucumbers, juicy tomatoes and thick yogurt we had selected from the breakfast buffet. We carried our trays to long tables to sit with other members of the kibbutz, trying to talk over the din of hundreds of clinking utensils. Joel and I were quiet while Frank chatted in Hebrew.

Afterward we walked the grounds, past rusty bicycles parked near houses. We saw the koi that were raised at Gan Shmuel then exported to Japan. Frank later arranged a summer experience for my nephew, Steven, so that he could live on the kibbutz and help in the koi department.

We toured orange groves that supplied the fruit to make concentrated orange juice the kibbutz shipped around the world. Frank was interested in this area because he had sold Gan Shmuel its first evaporator that removed water in order to condense the juice. I noticed barbed wire surrounding the outside of the kibbutz near the orange trees.

"It keeps strangers from taking our oranges," Gidi said, dismissing any sign of real danger with a wave of his hand.

In the nightclub—a bomb shelter with a door made out of strips of beads—Frank met someone from his Larchmont synagogue. It wasn't the first time he met an acquaintance in an unusual place. As Michael Levy once told me, "Wherever we go, my father always runs into people he knows."

One year a client who recycled used clothing invited Frank to go fishing in a remote part of northern California. The two men never caught anything, but in the midst of the pristine environment, Marty Silver, Frank's friend from high school in the Bronx, the one who had lost his dad's ring, jumped out of the woods and embraced Frank with a big hello. Marty had heard Frank speaking, recognized his accent and knew he had found his old friend.

On a business trip to Paris, Frank stayed at the hotel nursing a cold while I worked, shopped and visited The Louvre. At breakfast, when he felt better, I bubbled about how beautiful and elegant the French women were.

"They even wear silk scarves to shop at the butcher," I said.

"Where?" Frank asked. "Show me a beautiful woman."

"Right behind you," I said. "That woman with the scarf looks like the actress, Catherine Deneuve."

Frank turned his head. The woman looked at him and said, "Frank! Frank Levy. What are you doing here?"

It was one of his old girlfriends. I learned early in our relationship that Michael L. was right. Frank meets somebody he knows wherever we go. That's why I wasn't surprised he had found an old buddy in the kibbutz bomb shelter.

In Israel we hiked Masada at 6:00 AM to see the sunrise that had cast a red glow over the Moab Mountains in nearby Jordan. We floated in the Dead Sea with our legs bobbing because of the high concentration of salt in the water. We toured the Old City of Jerusalem, the holy site of the Western Wall and Yad Vashem, the Center for Holocaust Research. In Tel Aviv we swam in the Mediterranean Sea and visited the Diaspora Museum.

Of course we visited Bat Yam. It was nothing like the village where Frank grew up with no more than 2,000 residents and nothing like the place he returned to with Margit. That place no longer existed. When we walked along Balfour Street where Frank used to live, we wandered into a bustling city with over 130,000 people, including new Jewish immigrants from Turkey, the Soviet Union and Ethiopia in addition to Muslims and Christians.

A promenade along the sea housed pubs and restaurants. Many modern buses connected Bat Yam with other cities. Apartment buildings and houses were crowded together and Frank's school had more than doubled in size. Frank pointed out the hill that edged the promenade near the sea.

"It was the same hill where British soldiers used to sit in order to shoot over swimmers' heads into the water," he said.

Amongst all the history lessons and moments with Chezzi's family, Joel kept looking at art. He checked out the work of Frank's friend, Perli Pelzig, an internationally known painter, sculptor and mosaic artist. Joel examined pottery, considered small carpets and touristy souvenirs in the *souk*, the Arab market running through the Christian and Muslim quarters of Jerusalem's Old City. He wandered in and out of galleries in Jaffa on the way to Bat Yam. It wasn't until he stepped into a gallery near the King David Hotel that he saw a lithograph he loved. Joel admired the artwork for some time, but it was beyond his budget.

Frank realized how much Joel wanted this work of art, but didn't want to override my gift by adding more money. Instead, he tracked down the artist, Shraga Weil, at HaOgen, a kibbutz in Sharon Plain northeast of Tel Aviv. It was the same kibbutz where Frank's nephew, Josh, had worked on an archaeological dig for six months in 1985. Weil is famous for his painted door panels at the Kennedy Center's Israeli Lounge. His work is part of the permanent collections at Harvard and the Los Angeles County Museum.

Frank called Weil and convinced him to allow us to visit his cramped workspace. The print Joel liked was part of a triptych, three panels that can hang together or, in this case, alone. After watching Joel agonize for two hours over which piece to buy, we left with a signed artist proof of the print Joel had seen in the gallery.

"Frank doesn't go out of his way to make people happy," Joel said. "It *is* his way to make people happy."

Frank then shared a parable his father used to tell. It was an interpretation of a biblical story in which Jacob asks each of his 12 sons to bring one stick and then break it. The sons found the task easy. Next Jacob asks his sons to each gather another stick and bundle them together. The sons couldn't break the sticks.

Frank shared this tale because it illustrated the importance of unity and family. He then purchased Weil's other two prints that were part of the triptych: one for Joel's sister, Morgan, for her bat mitzvah and one for Joel's brother, Michael M. Frank hoped the connected art would be a symbol of family unity among my ex husband's three children.

A few years later Israel became another shared memory when Frank and I brought Michael Levy and his girlfriend, Jodi, to attend the wedding of Chezzi's daughter, Ofrit. Michael carried an engagement ring in his pocket. He planned to propose to Jodi on the beach in Bat Yam but was too excited to wait until we got there. We had started our trip in Eilat—a resort along the Red Sea not far from Petra in Jordan. One morning, as we walked toward our table to join the "kids" for breakfast, I noticed that Jodi was hiding her left hand in her lap.

"I think they're engaged," I said, but Frank wanted to fill his plate with fresh vegetables, fish, hummus and pita bread from the sumptuous buffet breakfast before we joined the young couple.

Even though the revelation was delayed a few minutes, it was still a joyous shared memory.

37: Think Sideways

2001 Terrorists attack the World Trade Center in New York City

2005 September: Largest UN world summit establishing millennium development goals, which included environment, social equity and economic demands.

In 2000 Frank received a phone call from Georgia Institute of Technology in Atlanta. Some professors knew that Frank and Sergio Dell'Orco were experts in recycling textile waste and used clothing. The professors wanted to challenge Frank and Sergio to think differently, to shift their knowledge to recycling used carpets.

At that time carpet manufacturers ground up post consumer carpets. By not separating the nylon from the backing, these people lost the ability to reuse the more valuable nylon that was a derivative of oil. If they could reprocess the nylon, their waste could become a profit center. It was an exciting concept so even though the lecture was presented in an academic setting, executives from many of the large carpet companies attended.

"The audience was talking about sustainability of resources, managing ecosystems, saving energy and responsibility for the environment," Frank said. "It was the first time we heard the word 'sustainability,' even though we had been immersed in the concepts behind recycling materials. Still, we didn't quite know what this word meant or that it was a more politically correct label for the work we had been doing for over 20 years."

Carpets present significant hazards to the environment. If dumped into landfills, they can fill an excavated hole one mile by one mile by 100 feet deep every year. If incinerated, the carpets release toxic chemicals. They are not biodegradable: So if accumulated, they never disintegrate.

"We wanted to solve this problem," Frank said. "But shifting from machinery that processed used clothing to machinery that processed post consumer carpets would not be so simple."

Sergio specialized in building opening lines, blending equipment and presses. If a customer needed a machine he didn't make, he partnered with other Italian machinery manufacturers in the Tuscan area to create turnkey operations. But Sergio didn't make machines that recycled carpets. Nobody knew how to make that kind of equipment. There was nobody with whom he could partner.

In addition, if Sergio and Frank shifted their business to the carpet industry, their customer base would be completely different. In the year 2000 they worked with entrepreneurs who collected tons of used clothing. The factory owners kept huge buildings to house tables used to sort clothes into about 220 different categories—everything from ties to t-shirts, as well as from trousers to shirts. Their facilities also had well-lit workspaces, continuous air conditioning and a fully automated processing system that controlled the movement of the clothing.

Once the used clothing was sorted, it had to be cut into pieces and steamed in order to kill 98% of the bacteria. Next fibers needed to be opened before adding liquids such as fire retardants and anti-bacterial treatments. At the end of these transactions there was still about 20% of material waste that could be restored to fiber.

"It's like mixing ingredients for a cake," Frank said, "with used clothing fibers being the flour."

Recycling clothing was complicated, well organized and well tested over time but it didn't apply to carpets. A different technology had to be created. New machinery had to be built. During that particular Q & A he and Sergio realized they needed to find a way to separate the carpet fiber from the backing.

"We knew it could be a good business and it would help save landfills," Frank said.

Sergio and Frank sat down with pencil and paper. It would take them six years to develop a technology to solve this complicated problem. A technology they could patent.

38: Breaking Bread Together

2005 Crivitz, Germany holds a 750-year anniversary.

"Who ordered duck and who ordered rabbit?" the waiter asked in German at the Hotel Haus Seeblick in Crivitz north of Berlin.

"I asked for only vegetables," I said to Frank. "I don't want duck."

"I ordered vegetables for you," Frank said. "The waiter brought you duck anyway. Please take it."

"I'll just eat the red cabbage and potatoes," I whispered. When we travel, I often become a temporary vegetarian. My culinary taste is simple. I prefer a peanut butter and jelly sandwich to local dishes. Our daughter-in-law, Jennifer, compares Frank to a complex dish that is both spicy and sweet with enough heat to intrigue but not overwhelm the palate, a culinary enigma who will try any food. He was delighted to eat rabbit.

The restaurant was in a stately red brick building in the midst of a lush forest overlooking a big lake. Sparse rooms with linoleum floors and Formica tables housed hunting, sailing, fishing and swimming trophies on dusty

227

shelves. Only our table was set with a white tablecloth, burgundy napkins and small vases with yellow flowers.

"I'm sure my grandfather had once belonged to the same lodge," Frank said. "Most likely dancing with my grandmother in the back room."

I wondered if in their day the menu had offered the same extra dark, gamey meat and dumplings that sat heavily on our plates. Frank was concerned about insulting our group if I didn't eat enough. He coaxed me to try some. Just some.

"How can you care if you insult these people?" I asked putting down my fork and looking at everyone around the table. "You realize their relatives probably were Nazis. Their parents most likely participated in Kristallnacht, running through the streets smashing windows of shops owned by Jews—including your great grandfather's department store right here in town. Maybe they also smashed the heads of some of your family. How can you sit with these people and break bread?"

I stared at Frank, relentless in my criticism. It didn't help that I was the only one on this excursion who did not understand German. I had lots of time to watch the people's weathered faces and live in my imagination.

"Maybe their ancestors sent your relatives to the gas chambers or made lampshades out of their skin," I said. "I don't care if they're insulted because I don't eat their disgusting duck. And why are you paying for this meal?"

"I'm thrilled to be here," Frank said. "I remember my grandfather with much love. He had studied weaving before he joined the German army and before he married and moved to Berlin. It is exciting to be where he grew up, where my maternal great grandparents had once strolled and where I once returned with my mother back in 1984."

We were a group of nine people—five from Germany, Frank and me and Frank's sister, Ada, and her husband, Don, who had traveled with us. Just a few hours before we all had walked the streets and viewed the brick and stucco houses that still lined wide cobblestone sidewalks, some with benches where residents could rest and visit with their neighbors.

Before our departure from the States, Frank had called the town historian, a second-generation veterinarian, Dr. Fritz Rohde, to tell him of our planned visit. Crivitz was celebrating its 750th anniversary and the village had just printed a 400-page book about all their citizens including the Jacobson family. Dr. Rohde was interested in any details Frank and Ada could share about their mother, Hilda Pauline Jacobson Levy and the rest of the Jacobson family.

A formal meeting was arranged to share information about Crivitz, the lives of its residents, what had happened to the town's Jews in WWII and how shocked the people were that their country had embraced the Holocaust. Members of the local government expressed happiness that Jewish people were returning.

"The warm reception from the six people in the German welcoming committee was more than any of us expected," Frank said.

As my brother, Jerry, and his wife, June, say, "Frank is the kind of person whom everyone automatically likes when they meet him. He is an interested, patient listener."
The committee's enthusiasm made me feel uncomfortable. I hoped it was because people gravitate to Frank rather than because we are Jewish.

Hartmunt Paulson, Town Director of Order and Social Affairs, had organized the morning meeting and midday meal. Historian Dieter Conell, who had fled west to Hamburg when the Russians swallowed up Crivitz, had moved back to Crivitz after the reunification of Germany. Fritz Rohde brought his wife, Inge.

Dr. Rathke, a tall thin man with gray hair, represented the local church. He was influential in finding out crimes the Stasi Secret Police of the East German government had committed. The Stasi had recruited East German citizens into becoming informants on their family and neighbors. We were told that based on Rathke's evidence, some members of the secret police had been put on trial.

The sixth person on the welcoming committee was an architect who narrated historical facts about the local buildings during our walking tour. He did not stay for lunch.

All these Germans had families that had lived in Crivitz for many generations. Dr. Rohde resided in the same house for over 80 years. Everyone in this group was Christian.

Inside the Town Hall a conference table was filled with historical books, maps and new published materials about Crivitz. A few other employees joined us. Everyone was friendly yet formal and polite. The Germans again mentioned Alfred Jacobson, Hilda's uncle, who had run the Jacobson Department Store started by Frank's great grandfather Eduard Jacobson.

In WWI, 20% of the German army was Jewish. Alfred was one of those soldiers. He died in 1918, a fallen war hero defending Germany in France. Five years later, in 1923, his wife, Ida, married Alfred's cousin, Hugo Lowenstein. Together they ran the general house ware and textile store they renamed L. Jacobson.

After the meeting at Town Hall, which lasted about 90 minutes, Dr. Rohde and two others escorted us on another walking tour of town. We saw the Jacobson home that had been situated above their general store. We passed a private house that had once been a synagogue. In Poland a similar synagogue that had been destroyed was restored. In Crivitz there was only a small plaque on a stake in the sidewalk that indicated this private home had once been a Jewish house of worship.

Prior to immigrating to Palestine, Frank's grandfather had been able to purchase the silver breastplate that decorated the Torah. He also bought two ornamental silver bells that sit on top of the Torah. These treasures stayed in Hilda's house until she gave them to Frank who later gave them to his younger son, David.

"I remembered that on my first trip to Crivitz years ago my mom had reconnected with Gerda Dumpelfeld. Unbeknownst to my sister and me," Frank said, "they corresponded for years. Dr. Rohde had acquired some of Hilda's letters and had incorporated our family information into the Crivitz 750th anniversary book."

Hilda's letters had been typed on an old German portable typewriter on thin airmail paper. She wrote: "Our family members were all good decent citizens and believed they belonged to the German nation. One can only imagine with difficulty that one does not really have a fatherland anymore."

"It was astounding to see a whole page on my life," Frank said. "My children, my career, our house in Larchmont. I had trouble grasping that this information had been printed up well before our visit, before my initial phone call."

The book also included a detailed description of Ada's family—that she and her husband are research scientists and had raised their boys, Josh and Barak, in Oakridge, Tennessee, before moving to Maine.

"It was strange to think that while we were looking for our roots," Frank said, "perhaps the people of this town were looking for their citizens whom they had failed."

Frank hoped I could see that despite all the evil, there were some human beings who tried to do the right thing and who also were victims of the Holocaust in a different way.

Next on our tour was the church where a list of fallen soldiers was carved into a plaque hanging on the stone wall. Among the town heroes was Hilda's uncle Alfred who had been killed defending Germany in WWI.

An important part of our walk was along the river where residents had washed their clothes until May 1964, when running water was installed throughout the town. The small waterway spread out to a beautiful lake where townspeople ice-skated in the winter, just as Frank's grandfather had done.

"I recalled the stories *opi* Martin told me when I was a little boy," Frank said, "He held a bed sheet he borrowed from the store. It caught the wind so he could skate fast enough to visit other towns along the lake. In my mind it was a peaceful, pristine scene."

During lunch at the lake house, Dr. Rohde slipped out briefly to drive home. He rushed back clutching a treasure, a photo of the L. Jacobson General store. It had been hanging on his wall and Fritz wanted Frank to see it. Frank's great grandfather was visible sitting in the window.

Later, Dr. Rohde told Frank a little more of his memories from his youth. Frank translated for me.

"On Kristallnacht," Rohde said, "windows were completely banged apart in the L. Jacobson store. Then signs were posted on the store telling people not to buy anything from the Jews, not to work for the Jews. Some customers came in from the back, over the brook, so SA guards were stationed there to cover both entrances. Loyal men and women had the courage to go against the terror of the mob of the street and went inside anyway.

"Hugo Lowenstein was the second husband of your mother's aunt. He was a middle-to-large person with a quiet deep voice and very good manners toward his clients who would come to buy suits for their family's confirmation. If a customer didn't have much money, Hugo would tell him, pay when you can. In the Christmas season Hugo received his customers with a cup of coffee and a piece of *topfkuchen*, a ribbed cake baked in the kitchen behind the offices.

"After Kristallnacht, Hugo went to Town Hall. He came back destroyed psychologically. Neighbors could hear him yelling to Ida, 'There is no use! There is no use! We are not allowed to sell anymore!'

"Very soon both of them disappeared. They left everything behind. Before leaving they said goodbye to a few friends and the Koch family who owned the bakery. They gave the Kochs their sterling sliver coffee pot and matching sugar and creamer."

"Listening to Fritz all I could think of were my parents," Frank said. "I had newfound respect for them leaving everything familiar in Germany in 1936. I was grateful and in awe that my folks had been able to bring my grandparents to Palestine. For the first time, I was aware of the horror my new German friends had felt watching the ramifications of Hitler's final solution play out in their town."

By now everyone at lunch was very relaxed. Dessert was served—a thick pudding with *schlag*, heavy whipped cream. Frank was relieved that I had given up control over menu selection and just said thank you. As I looked at the white dishes on the table I thought about the porcelain white dishes Hilda's mother, Marta, somehow had managed to bring to Palestine and then to America. I am happy they are with Michael Levy and his wife, Jodi, a daily link to the past.

During dessert, Dr. Rohde whispered to Frank, "I wrote my own memoir. I included your mother's letters because they are strong proof of our being connected and the deep heartfelt feelings of human beings of extreme pleasantness despite all that has happened to your people because of our horror. My wife and I went to America in 1996," he added. "If I had known about these letters, I would have visited Dr. Hilda Levy. I am sure we would have met and had much to say to each other."

One year later Frank's sister received an old wooden hanger that said Jacobson. It had been used in the Jacobson department store. Shortly after, Frank received the 80-page memoir from Dr. Rohde that included details from their private conversations. Dr. Rohde wrote:

> One foggy night Mr. Franz Erdman took the Lowenstein couple secretly, in his Opal car, to Hamburg. It was a very brave and dangerous thing for Mr. Erdman to do. When one of Ida Lowenstein's neighbors in Crivitz later met her in Hamburg, Ida was wearing a yellow star. The neighbor was happy to see her, but Ida warned, 'You are bringing yourself into big danger if you are seen talking to me.'
>
> Not long after that brief encounter, we heard that Hugo and Ida were rounded up and sent to Buchenwald, a concentration camp near Weimar where the famous German poets

Goethe and Schiller came from. The Lowensteins were murdered in Buchenwald.

The Nazis took over their store in Crivitz and later a Nazi's son ran the store. After the war ended in 1945 he committed suicide. Many Germans committed suicide at that time, perhaps because they were afraid to be known for war crimes they had committed.

When the East German Deutsche Democratic Republic (DDR) came to power, yet another person took over the store that still exists on Parchimerstrasse #12. Under the DDR it was called The Fashion House of Crivitz.

In 1942, Dr. Otto Ladevig, who worked at the local bank and had a small manufacturing operation, was the last Jew in Crivitz. We don't know what happened to his brother, the lawyer in Hamburg, or his other brother, the doctor in Berlin. Otto was a bachelor who liked to go to Hotel Rover in Crivitz and have a coffee in the early evening. He was friendly with everyone. One day he went home and hung himself by his suspenders.

I was shocked to hear about it because just a few days earlier we had shared a conversation while walking along a path with beautiful roses. Otto must have known he would soon be rounded up and could not stand the frights, the shocks and tortures that he would surely face.

"While reading the memoir I believed nothing could be more chilling," Frank said. "Then I read Rohde's newest entry and was so disheartened."

Fritz wrote:

Years ago I would have absolutely believed it is impossible that once again in my lifetime I would be confronted in my land with the neo-Nazis and the brutality of the skinheads. In the nearby town of Schwerin I saw young people, boys and girls, in familiar Nazi uniform parading in front of the Schwerin Schloss (castle). I really could not imagine this happening again.

This reinforces my belief that we cannot ignore the social questions of responsible nationalism. I am shocked that the neo-Nazis exist at all and I am horrified at this re-emerging right radicalism in our country as well as other countries.

One cannot take for granted the social complex problem existing amongst our youth. We must take the young people seriously. Older people look at younger ones with a cold attitude, not understanding them, not seeing that they are the children of our society but we must not allow ourselves to just look at them and not know what to do with their energies. How else will our youth know what we all have lived through? How else will they know what to do if they have no jobs and they haven't learned anything and we don't try to help them in the family, in the schools? When we talk to them it should not just be empty words.

Now it is over half a century since the end of WWII. It is a very long time, yet the memories of this era are very close, as if I had only seen them a short while ago. The older I become, the more intensely I think about those times, the more I understand that the memories and the individual details show slices and points that up to today become the most important experiences of life. I did not recognize them at that time. Mostly I just had a negative feeling.

The memories of the last days of the Third Reich are in my mind as a dream as far away as the Alps. They have stayed with me my whole life. They are painful memories of a terrible, terrible war that in the name of the German nation, in a sick way, moved over the nations of Europe. In 1994 my wife and I traveled to Israel and to Yad Vashem. Crivitz had Jews since 1574. I can't understand how this happened. I am ashamed as a German for what was done to the Jews but one can't change the mosaic of our time.

"I always felt that one can't blame all Germans, especially those who were not old enough to participate in the military during the Hitler era," Frank said. "I even admire German efficiency and orderly productivity. Maybe sharing the details of an innocent German's reality during this time can help bridge our cultures. Maybe Chezzi's work in Israel with the children of the Holocaust will ease the healing."

Before we parted from Crivitz, I watched Fritz and Frank—two new friends hug—a big bear hug.

"It is comforting to know that at least one person, Dr. Rohde, feels remorse and shares our pain," Frank said, "and there must be others. Yet, whatever conclusions I draw," he said, "they all seem naïve and empty."

39: Reparations

*1953   West Germany agreed to pay Israel for the slave
        labor and persecution of Jews during the Holocaust
        and to compensate Jews for property that was stolen
        by the Nazis. West Germany paid Israel three billion
        marks over the next 14 years.*

*The Conference on Jewish Material Claims Against
Germany.*

*1966   The Luxemburg Agreement obligated the West
        German government to pay Israel three billion
        deutsche marks ($1.85 billion) and another 450
        million Deutsch marks ($292 million) to Jewish
        organizations.*

After the war Germany accepted responsibility for the
Holocaust atrocities. The government agreed to pay
restitution to survivors of those who were persecuted.

"You have to understand," Frank said. "It wasn't so
simple."

Many relatives of the victims argued that accepting
reparation payments was like forgiving the Nazis. Others

felt payments were due to families who had lost everything they owned. Still others believed the money should go to Israel to help build the land and pay for the estimated 500,000 Holocaust survivors absorbed by the young country.

Both individuals and Israel were given reparations. The monies Israel received were used to pay for electric power plants, war ships, highways, trains, a pipeline to enable the Negev desert to have water for plants to bloom and to support many other segments of the country's infrastructure.

Chezzi's brother was able to get a painting back. Uncle Herbert and Frank's father also tried to get reimbursed for the Berthold Levy Printing Company. When Frank's grandfather died, the company passed on to his wife, Alice, the grandmother who is credited with bringing the Levy family together in America. According to German law, upon Alice's death, the company went equally to her two sons, Uncle Herbert and Frank's dad, Fred.

"As long as my father was alive, I didn't think about restitution," Frank said. "I don't know what my dad and Herbert did or what correspondence they had with the German government. Despite their efforts, nothing happened."

After Frank's dad died Hilda received $678.96 every month, most likely because Fred had worked in Germany from 1923 to 1936. Her payments emphasized the good records the Germans kept and their intention to compensate their citizens.

Years later, when Frank became the eldest male in the Levy clan, he accepted responsibility for securing restitution payments for the family business. He wrote letters, hired an attorney and followed up with calls and more letters.

By now Hilda was in her early 90s. She worked with Frank longer than she had been married to her husband. She still wore high heels and business suits. She dyed her hair brown and maintained an elegant, formal German style.

"Every one of my suppliers and clients knew her," Frank said.

Despite macular degeneration that limited her vision in the center of her visual field, she walked over a mile from her apartment to Frank's home office. When she came to a traffic light on the corner, she pushed the walk button and waited for a buzzing sound that indicated the walk sign was stopping traffic.

Frank was able to obtain a special machine from Lighthouse International in New York City. It enabled her to continue to read letters and business documents. She spent many hours corresponding with friends and distant relatives in Israel, Germany, France and South Africa, switching from one language to the next as easily as someone switches from a fork to a spoon. As she got older one friend, then another passed away until she was the only one left in her age group. She kept up relationships through lengthy phone calls to the next generation. Hilda also followed the reparation saga, encouraging Frank to continue his efforts.

It wasn't until she turned 93 that her memory began to fade. She lost the ability to take the local train to Manhattan. She stopped coming to the office. She became homebound around the same time my mother became bedridden with spinal stenosis and suffered from Alzheimer's. For the next few years we took care of both of them while they remained in their separate homes.

At the end Hilda no longer remembered who I was though she maintained a polite welcome when I brought her weekly supply of groceries. I always included big bags of chocolate that she and Frank consumed on his daily visits.

Hilda passed away on February 13, 2003. Ada's son, Barak, gave a moving speech at her funeral. The Levys received their restitution payment three years later.

"On behalf of my sister and my cousins, as well as myself, I was able to get compensated for the 60% of the printing plant the family still owned when the Nazis confiscated it. I was sorry my mother couldn't know about this token."

"How do you repay families for the loss of their loved ones, their friends, their way of life, the futures they planned?" I kept asking Frank.

"For most of the victims and their families, there is no redemption," he said.

40: Finding Cousin Benas

*1994 South Africa holds its first universal elections since
the end of Apartheid. Neslon Mandela becomes
President.*

Frank resembles his distant cousin, Benas Levy. They have
the same full lips, the same brown hair and the same walk.
Their sons are both tall and thin with dark brown eyes and
dark curly hair. The two fathers look like brothers. Maybe
it's because their great grandfathers were brothers.

Frank can trace his ancestors to 1740. One of those
was Simon Levy who had eight children. Frank is part of a
branch from one of those eight; Benas from another. As a
result of Hitler, most Levys scattered to Palestine, London,
America, South Africa and Australia.

In 1933 Benas's father, Heine, moved from
Germany to Holland where he met Benas's mother. Due to
the ominous developments preceding WWII they
immigrated to South Africa five years later. Separated by
distance and cultures, the two arms of the same ancestors
lost track of each other. To Frank, they became one of the
misplaced families mentioned in Holocaust articles.

"We always wondered what happened to that Levy," Frank said. "My father assumed his cousin had been killed by the Nazis."

Imagine Frank's surprise when Benas visited him and Margit in New York in 1984.

"I didn't know about him," Frank said. "I only knew that there were missing cousins."

Benas explained that eight months after he was born, his father died. His mother eventually remarried. A few years later she also passed away, leaving Benas, age 14, and his half sister, age 8. Benas went to boarding school. His sister, Judy, remained with her father. Benas's mom left him an extensive stamp collection.

"One stamp was glued to an envelope that had the name Ernst Levy and a London address," Benas said. Ernst also was a descendent of Simon Levy. "Years later after I was married and had a good job, I flew to London on a business trip. Of course I looked up Ernst. He was the first relative on my father's side I knew as an adult. Ernst told me to contact Herbert, Frank's uncle. It was Herbert who put me in touch with Frank."

"Though I grew up with a small family," Frank said, "There were many relatives and I was thrilled to unite with some of them."

In comparison, my mother had 51 first cousins in the Metropolitan New York area. I remember their monthly cousins club meetings as joyous, food-filled events with accordion music and tambourines. Everyone gorged on lox and bagels while smoking and yelling in English with a smattering of Yiddish words. As they aged the men became louder and the women turned blonder. The cousins all knew each other and I grew up with the next generation. We never spoke about missing relatives.

Once united, Benas and Frank stayed in touch. Frank's first trip to Johannesburg was to attend the bar mitzvah of Benas's son, Jonathan.

"At the gala Benas introduced me as the first member of his family who was celebrating an event with him," Frank said.

As a young adult Jonathan visited New York. At the airport I spotted him right away because he looked so much like David. In 2006 Frank and I flew to Cape Town to attend Jonathan's wedding. One of Jonathan's three sisters, Kathy, and her husband, Simon, settled in New York. They have shared several Thanksgiving feasts with us.

41: Saving The Land

2004 The pan-European Green Party, dedicated to environmental responsibility, sustainable development, social justice and pacifism, is established in Rome.

2008 The Israeli Green Party is formed.

Ever since Frank and Sergio gave their presentation at the Georgia Institute of Technology, they had been experimenting with machines and combined processes to solve the carpet waste dilemma.

"We couldn't forget that two and a half million tons of used carpets are dumped into U.S. landfills annually," Frank said. "Laid flat, *Choose Green Report* claims that the carpets would cover an area the size of New York City. Most carpets in the United States are nylon based, which means petroleum based."

If they could reprocess the nylon, the energy saved with a single line of recycling machinery would correspond to the heating demand of an estimated 250 U.S. households with about 200,000 barrels of oil saved per year per. By 2006, Frank and Sergio had solved the problem.

"We created a unique system to separate the nylon fibers from the polypropylene backing," Frank said.

They immediately formed a company, Post Consumer Carpet Processing Technologies® (PCC®), applied for a patent and reached out to entrepreneurs who wanted to recycle post-consumer carpets.

"You can't imagine how excited we were," Frank said, "that each line of our equipment could reclaim up to 30 million pounds of used carpet every year."

To accomplish this goal, a factory owner must first purchase a line of approximately 17 different machines that cost anywhere from three to five million dollars. The line has to be able to process a variety of carpets regardless of whether they contain synthetic fibers, wool or blends.

So much equipment demands a building of about 80,000 square feet with a number of loading docks. Location also is important. A carpet recycling factory is more successful if it is near at least two million people because the more people who live or visit an area, the more carpets are consumed.

"You have to understand," Frank said, "it's not so simple. Renting space on the East or West Coast is expensive, but it's where much carpet is located. In the more rural areas factory space costs less, but there are fewer used carpets so a business owner would have to pay to truck carpets to the waste recycling plant."

Of course, there are exceptions. Las Vegas is a prime location because it has numerous hotels and trade shows and therefore often replaces carpets. Best of all is Atlanta where more than half the carpet companies in the USA are within a 65-mile radius of Dalton, Georgia, not far from Atlanta. In December 2006 PCC® partnered with one of those companies, Interface.

In 1973, Ray C. Anderson, founded Interface, Inc. The company produced the first free-lay carpet tiles in

America. If one tile becomes stained or has a cigarette burn, the owner can replace just that tile rather than carpet covering the floor of the entire hotel room, lobby, airport corridor or restaurant. Carpet tiles revolutionized the commercial floor covering business. InterfaceFLOR became the world's largest manufacturer of modular carpets and Interface, Inc. became the third largest carpet manufacturer in America.

"Ray had a vision," Frank said. "He wanted to eliminate all negative impacts his company might have on the environment. His leadership in mission zero sustainability made Interface the most logical first partner for PCC®."

In his book, *Confessions of a Radical Industrialist,* Anderson discussed sustainability, indicating that it is both the right and the smart thing to do. When it came to carpets, it could be argued that each pound of nylon carpet contains the energy equivalent of more than a gallon of regular unleaded gasoline.

To reach carpet manufacturers, Frank and Sergio attended a Carpet America Recovery Effort (CARE) gathering. CARE is an organization dedicated to finding "market-based solutions to recycle post-consumer carpets." At the CARE meeting in Georgia, Frank dropped a bag of white fiber on the table in front of Stuart Jones, Interface's Vice President for Research. The label read: "Post Consumer Recycled Nylon." The material looked new and Jones was intrigued.

Frank called a meeting in Riverhead, New York, and invited Jones and a few other people from the carpet industry to discuss the PCC® technology. Among the group was Brendan McSheehy, Vice President, Director of Research and Development of Universal Fibers, leaders in colorful, high-quality fibers, including post-consumer nylon 6 that combines forms of plastic with textile fibers. Universal Fibers is also committed to a better environment and actively participates in the Carpet America Recovery Effort.

At the conclusion of the Riverhead meeting, Brendan put his arm around Frank and said, "This is the most exciting thing I have seen. Tomorrow I shall arrange for you to have a phone call from your new partners."

The next day Frank spoke with Eric Nelson, Vice President of Interface who immediately flew up to New York from Georgia.

"About a week later," Frank said, "along with three executives from Interface, we were viewing the equipment in Sergio's factory in Italy."

After watching the machines in action, Eric was convinced PCC® and Interface were a good match.

"As I stood there and watched the old carpet being fed into the machines, I was amazed at what was coming out the other side—carpet nylon clean enough to be remade into new carpet fiber. I knew this was truly a game-changing innovation."

Soon after signing a nondisclosure agreement, a licensing agreement and contracts, they set up the first line in LaGrange, Georgia. While Interface reuses the nylon from the carpets, the materials also can be formed into pellets and mixed with plastic for products such as telephone handles, computer cabinets and dashboards for cars.

Later that year PCC® was selected out of 853 sustainability projects from 109 countries as the winner of the World ENERGY GLOBE Award for the United States. PCC® also was one of three finalists for an additional prize in the Energy category.

"With this recognition," Frank said, "maybe other companies and governments will be influenced to clean up the Earth. I was happy to fulfill my lifelong dream to help save the land and proud that our green project could help our planet."

"I was beyond proud to be an American, winning for my adopted country."

42: Shopping In Italy

*1980s   Chinese immigrants begin to settle in Prato, Italy,
producing garments made in Italy by Chinese
laborers earning low wages. Chinese transform
parts of the Prato textile center into an area that
makes low-end garments.*

*2007   Chinese immigrants pour into Prato, Italy, the
country's main textile manufacturing center. Some
are there illegally. The unlawful competition forces
many Italian textile businesses to close.*

"I want to share my experiences in Italy with our
daughters-in-law," I said when Frank asked me what I
wanted for my 65th birthday.

"Are you sure you wouldn't prefer a new piece of
jewelry?" he asked.

"No jewelry," I said. "You bought me enough and I
wear my favorite necklace and earrings almost every day.
That's all I need."

"How about a party?" he asked.

"No party," I said.

At the ad agency I had created events all the time—from formal dinners for the international executives to galas for hundreds of employees and clients. For my birthday I envisioned a shared memory far more dear to my heart: a shopping spree in Italy with the girls.

For 15 years I had been accompanying Frank on business trips to Prato, outside of Florence. We had watched Sergio's daughters grow up and we made friends with other suppliers and their families. We brought back clothes for our grown-up kids and grandchildren, told tales, showed photos and shared recipes from my favorite restaurants. Each time I stepped into a shop featuring outfits for younger women and colorful sweaters for guys, I longed for our grown children to be in Italy to select something special. When I walked by an ice-cream stand with *nocciola* flavored *gelato* or enjoyed pasta at a *ristorante* on a hill overlooking vineyards and olive groves, I dreamed the rest of our family could soak it up with us.

"During meals with the younger generation of machine suppliers," Frank said, "I wished I could connect our lives much like we did with our blended family."

Over the years we have taken the boys on a few extraordinary excursions, including skiing in Cortina with a stop in Venice during *Carnivale* and a reunion with the DeMas family with whom I had lived in nearby Belluno, Italy, thanks to a program called The Experiment in International Living (now World Learning). It was long ago, between my junior and senior years at college and the reunion was spectacular. Another time we also brought the "kids" to a machine show in Paris with a side trip to the French Riviera and, of course, a tour of Sergio's factory to help everyone see the machinery Frank sells.

"Our boys had done it all," Frank said. "It was the girls' turn to bond."

Frank organized three days near Florence and two days in Venice to tour the Biennale Art show. Michael

251

Levy's wife, Jodi, Joel's wife, Jen, and my Michael's girlfriend accepted our invitation. With three kids and a career as a pediatric oncologist, it was impossible to find a time when David's wife, Carolyn, could get free. Frank's niece-in-law, Naomi took her place and we gave Carolyn some cash to buy something for herself in New York.

Upon arriving at the *Amerigo Vespucci* Airport in Florence, Frank handed each girl a plain white number ten envelope that contained euros. The game was simple. Spend all of it on themselves during the next five days or return any remaining money at the end of the trip. I could feel their excitement as Sergio and his associate drove us to the Art Museo Hotel in Prato, about 14 kilometers west along the A11 motorway.

There are close to 200,000 residents in this sprawling city nestled beneath Monte Retaia in the Calvana chain of mountains in Tuscany. Inside the old town, the section surrounded by an ancient stonewall, the girls tried on shoes in the small shops. We munched on thin-crusted pizza and sampled robust Carmignano red wine, then tasted almond-flavored biscotti at the famous Antonio Mattei bakery. We stopped by the studio of our friend and photographer, Alessandro Moggi, on Via Garibaldi who our family friend, Valentina Ghioldi, had introduced us to years ago. Five years earlier Frank and I had hired Alessandro to take our photos in the hills of Tuscany. Since then he and his family visited us in the States.

The girls touched every blouse, pair of pants, sweater and belt in the boutiques along the narrow side streets. I followed close by because I planned to give the first purchaser an extra 50 euros, but nobody parted with a single bill. They worried they would find something better the next day in Florence. With no returns allowed and no time to revisit an area, the pressure to decide whether to buy or not to buy became gigantic.

"I can't believe everyone still has her cash," Frank said later that night at dinner.

On day two, after the best *cappuccino* at *La Tazza d'Oro* across from the hotel, we caught a bus into Florence. The bus stop was near the *Questura*, the police headquarters. Outside was a line of Chinese people. As we drove along the highway we could see factories with signs in Chinese and Italian.

Sergio later explained that since the late 1980's the Chinese have been immigrating to Prato. Now the city is home to perhaps the largest group of Chinese in Europe. Some claim the number is over 50,000 but that figure is hard to verify because many are illegal immigrants who work, eat and sleep in the textile manufacturing facilities and often don't get counted and are paid low wages. It is said that the Chinese owners almost always avoid taxes and they sell garments for much less than legitimate Italian enterprises do. At least that is what I have been told.

"And the tags say '*Made in Italy*,'" Sergio said.

Vans from retailers all over Europe come into the area to purchase these low-end garments. Sergio believes the system denigrates the fine reputation of clothing made in Italy by skilled Italian workers. The system has put many Italian family-owned companies out of business. Worse, with most Chinese groups not paying taxes unless the police raid a business, much of the profit is funneled back to China. Rumors claim the amount could be as high as $1.5 million per day.

"With thousands of registered businesses and factories in the area," Frank said, "the sporadic police raids are only a dent."

To accommodate the Chinese workers, Chinese restaurants, shops and schools have sprung up all over Prato, changing the core culture in some areas.

"That explains why there are always busloads of Chinese tourists at our hotel," I said.

"Not so," Sergio said. "In most cases the Asian tourists, as many as three to four buses at each hotel every night, are not from China. They are from Taiwan, Korea and Japan."

When we checked in to our hotel for our shopping spree our lobby was filled with Asian visitors. Even the public city bus to Florence included many Chinese passengers who spoke Italian. They are the new generation—people who came to Italy when they were two or three years old or who were born in Italy.

After visiting the Basilica di Santa Maria del Fiore (the Duomo) and the Baptistry of St. John with its famous Gates of Paradise (Golden Doors) we moved on to the nearby San Lorenzo Market to check out scarves, belts, leather goods and other small items. It was day two and still nobody had bought anything. Michael's girlfriend liked a carved wooden musical jewelry box. All four decided to buy one. Then nobody bought one.

An hour or two later Jodi was the first to acquire something, an inexpensive leather belt. The extra 50 euros were hers despite mock grumbles from the others. On *Via Tornabuoni* Naomi, the girl from Maine who favors L.L. Bean, went for a Max Mara designer jacket and a teal colored cashmere sweater. Jen, who likes athletic wear and feminine outfits, bought a black wool Max & Co. junior coat, but held onto a substantial amount of cash to buy fine leather boots at the outlet stores. Jodi, who usually prefers more trendy outfits and designer bags, chose an olive green quilted Max & Co. coat. Weeks later we had to order one in black to be shipped to Carolyn.

Nobody could make a selection without unanimous group approval. It was fun to watch the struggle. As the girls tried on coat after coat, blouse after blouse, trying to figure out which looked best, my mind drifted to Hilda and

Fred and their life and death choice to leave their homeland. How lucky we were to be together, faced with unimportant decisions of what to buy. I hoped Frank appreciated his grandmother Alice who had kept his family together and allowed him to grow up with his cousins. As quickly as these thoughts erupted, they disappeared and my mind refocused on our more frivolous adventure. I wonder how often Frank's past quietly pops into his present tense.

The next day, at the deeply discounted outlets, we shopped Prada, Gucci, Dior, Ferragamo. Jen bought her boots but everyone else still held tight to her envelope.

That afternoon we visited Sergio's factory, about the size of a football field with high ceilings. During the walk through the plant the girls were surprised at the cleanliness of the environment, the 20-foot high ceilings and the freshly painted machinery. Skylights were positioned to the north so there would never be direct sunlight or shadows in the workers eyes. The employees wore earplugs so the noise of soldering, hammering, grinding, sharpening, screeching and drilling was kept to a low din. I could smell burned steel.

The floor was made of extra hard tiles fashioned from quartz rather than cement. Boxes of gears, motor parts, over 200 different screws and brackets were stored on the side of the factory. Other areas contained tubular metal bars and platforms for bales. An overhead crane was used to transport steel shafts weighing 250 pounds each, then bundled to add up to six tons or the equivalent of three cars at one time.

The machines are computerized so the cylinders turn without vibrations. The completed machines are painted twice before being sent in large containers to customers.

"The paint is so smooth you can't tell where the parts have been welded," Frank said.

A second room adjacent to the factory had no heat and a lower ceiling. It was used to warehouse the machines before they were shipped to customers.

"It is a very precise business," Sergio said. "Every piece must be in the correct position and welded precisely so spare parts can fit in even though many are made by hand according to the special demands of each customer. Maybe the parts can fit in over 100 different ways."

Best of all were the workers who wore friendly smiles and the latest casual men's fashion even though they were inside a factory. Rubber aprons protected the front of their garments and gloves protected their hands. Some wore goggles. Others donned what appeared to be designer eyeglasses. Frank pointed to each piece of equipment with the pride of a father showing off his genius child.

Upstairs, in the executive wing, we spoke with Sergio's daughter, Dr. Sara Bernacchi and met Dr. Massimo Pisaneschi, Sergio's top assistant, as well as Simona, Sergio's secretary. Next we were whisked off to another facility to watch fabric torn into clips then opened into fiber, cleaned, fluffed and spit out again ready to be spun or pressed for nonwovens.

"So far the Chinese are not making competitive machinery in Prato," Frank said.

At dusk, Sergio and his wife Manuela and their family joined us up in the hills in Artimino, an ancient town where the Medici family once ruled. It is where our friend, the photographer Alessandro Moggi, had taken our photos. His wife, Susanna, and daughter, Eleonora, joined us too. The enormous Medici summer villa, *La Ferdinanda* (the Villa of One Hundred Chimneys) overlooks a 360-degree view of the countryside with acres of vineyards, olive groves and little towns centered around churches. At Da Delfina we ate *pappardelle* with wild boar *ragu*. Well, some of us ate it.

The next day we caught a high-speed train to Venice to view *La Biennale di Venezia,* a contemporary art exhibition that has taken place once every two years since 1895. It has grown and now includes art, architecture, dance, film, theater and music in venues throughout the city. But first we stopped at the *Piazza San Marco* where Frank had fed pigeons over 70 years earlier.

"I still remember my little black dog," he said. "The one Uncle Herbert bought me when we fled Germany on our way to Palestine—that souvenir I brought to America and later gave to my first grandson, Yoni."

We lingered awhile in the *Piazza* listening to music before catching the *vaporetto* to the *Giardini,* the park that housed 30 permanent national pavilions filled with art. All the girls had money left in their envelopes so on our way to the water taxi we stopped at Furla to look at handbags. Jen and Naomi each bought identical leather purses. Me, too. The first to use up her money was Jen. I gave her another 50 euros.

Meanwhile, Jodi debated about a purse. She held it by the mirror, checked the inside, put it down, picked it up, placed it on her shoulder and debated again. At the last minute she passed on the handbag. On the boat to the airport she returned 200 euros.

"That's how it is," Frank said. "Decisions one day affect actions the next."

Back home, Carolyn's daughter, Eliana, said that since her mother was given cash before the trip she spent her money first and finished spending her money first. According to the game we owed her mom another $100.

"More important," Frank said, "we connected my life's work with our family and created some wonderful shared memories."

43: An Award For America

1990 Mikhail Gorbachev wins the Nobel Peace Prize.

1991 Kofi Annan wins the Nobel Peace Prize.

2008 Barack Obama is elected President of the USA. He wins the Nobel Peace Prize a year later.

2008 German and Israeli cabinets meet in Israel in honor of Israel's 60th anniversary.

Smile. Flash. Snap. Next. The photographers were busy capturing each winner along with their friends and family as they entered the European Parliament building in Brussels. A red carpet covered the long corridor from the door to the open circular staircase, a work of art in its own right. A 30-foot high gold statue of a globe supported by a gold hand was placed at the base. Chandeliers illuminated the area casting a warm glow over everyone. It was the entrance to the World ENERGY GLOBE Award festivities and we felt like celebrities.

When friends talk about basketball players and gossiped about celebrities, Frank always wonders why engineers, whose work creates jobs and new technologies, never get equal acknowledgement. Today was their turn and Sergio and Frank were among those being honored. The recognition Frank had always sought for an engineer was happening.

"I wished I could tell Margit's mom," Frank said. "She always loved the Oscars and this event would have pleased her."

The World ENERGY GLOBE Award was started in 1999 to honor projects that make economical use of resources and employ alternative energy sources. That evening 15 awards were to be given out in five categories: Earth, Fire, Water, Air and Youth, as well as awards to the best project from each participating country. The event was to be broadcast by 256 international TV stations and online and was expected to reach 2.5 billion households.

Award presenters Kofi Annan, past Secretary-General of the United Nations and winner of the Nobel Peace Prize in 2001, Hans-Gert Pottering, President of the European Parliament, European Commission President Jose Manuel Barroso and European Commission head Janez Jansa, mingled with the crowd adding to the drama of the moment. At the event, Mikhail Gorbachev, past President of the Soviet Union and winner of the Nobel Peace Prize in 1990, received an honorary World ENERGY GLOBE Award.

While Frank chatted with Christoph Winterbacher, Project Manager for the World ENERGY GLOBE Award and producer of the National Energy Globe Award Ceremony as well as the evening Gala, my Michael let the rest of us in on his big secret. He had arranged for Chezzi to fly from Jerusalem to Brussels to attend the program.

Once we knew, Michael L. and I wouldn't leave Frank's side. We hovered around him, not wanting to miss the excitement when Frank spotted his childhood friend.

"I thought you were interested in everything I found worthwhile," Frank said to me later, "but you were only waiting to witness my reaction when I saw Chezzi."

In the main lobby were human sized posters describing each country's winning project. Frank and Sergio posed near theirs for more photos before Mrs. Maneka Gandhi, a member of the Indira Gandhi family, political activist and environmentalist, presented their award.

My Michael was busy snapping 2,000 photos, documenting every emotional moment. He was the first to see Chezzi and guided us toward him. Frank stared at Chezzi, trying to process what he saw, trying to figure out what his childhood friend was doing in the building.

"I was so shaken it was a good thing I did not have to make a speech," Frank said, "or I would have been lost in memories, teary-eyed and unable to connect with the audience. I could hardly believe I was in the EU, let alone with the man I had known in Palestine since I was eight years old," Frank said. "But there we were, one American, age 75, one Israeli, age 77, both from families that had fled Germany early enough to avoid the Holocaust, both immigrants in our adoptive lands."

Despite being separated by 7,000 miles and leading dramatically different lifestyles, before computers and cell phones, Frank and Chezzi had kept in close contact. Their grown children continued the friendship as if they were family living across the street.

"We used to wear shorts and sandals," Frank said. "Now Chezzi and I were facing each other wearing suits and leather shoes."

They stood together in front of a poster describing the PCC® project. Frank choked up. Tears dripped on to his new Ferragamo tie, the one I had bought for him for the gala that night.

"I couldn't understand why I was I crying," Frank said. "I was embarrassed to let Sergio and his wife Manuela see me like this."

Frank's son, Michael L., was smiling nearby in support of his dad. He had studied textiles at Clemson University and although he had shifted his career to real estate, he was familiar with all that Frank had done to receive this extraordinary recognition. An avid music fan, he also was looking forward to the gala when he would hear Dionne Warwick, Alanis Morissette and the popular Italian singer, Zucchero.

Our children and grandchildren, our cousins in Westchester, Margit's family in California, Ada and Don and their kids in Maine, my brother, Jerry, and his wife, June, in New York City all cheered us on from their homes, watching on their computers. I think Chezzi's kids, Yuval, Eldad, Gonan and Ofrit also were watching in Israel as was Gidi and his family in Gan Shmuel.

Wherever we walked inside the European Parliament building, cameras flashed, adding to the celebratory atmosphere. Some winners wore native costumes from parts of Africa, India and South America. Many other attendees were in evening gowns and tuxedoes, reminding me of the Oscars and Emmy's, shows I had often watched on television.

The awards ceremony in the plenary room had attracted over 1,000 people. We were ushered to reserved seats in front of TV cameras in the third row of long tables that were shaped in an arc just like the ones at the United Nations. Chezzi and our sons skipped the cocktail party to stay near the closed doors, ready to be among the first guests allowed to enter the room. They sat right behind Sergio, Manuela, Frank and me.

During the evening we met with Wolfgang Neumann, President of the ENERGY GLOBE Foundation. Amidst the thousand people milling about we also were able to meet some of the three finalists in each category: Earth, Air, Fire, Water and Youth. In addition to our winning award for technology developed in the United States, PCC® was a finalist in the Earth category, competing with Peru's project to collect garbage by bicycle and with Germany's prototype of a small village that is self-sustaining with natural resources. Each group of finalists had TV cameras focused on them, replaying on huge onstage screens. The kids at home saw us and were sure we would win.

The cameras were on us so we were surprised when Peru won. In hindsight we understood that their project could be reproduced all over Peru, thereby helping a large population to have a cleaner environment and cleaner water. Our project can help alleviate landfills especially in the United States, but only developed countries can afford the luxury of wall-to-wall carpets. We understood why we didn't come in first.

Over the past six decades Frank had traveled the globe on business seeing communities wasting or spoiling everything from water and electricity, forests and land to old clothes, textile scraps and old cars.

"My German upbringing never allowed me to throw anything away," he said, "not even a morsel of food. Maybe that is why it pained me so much to see people being careless about their natural resources."

With English as his third language, somehow his mechanical abilities and engineering degree had led him to the textile recycling industry where many generations of his family had earned their living. Along the way he developed lasting friendships that transcended manmade political differences. Many of these friends had wanted to attend the presentation in Brussels, but Frank had said no.

"If any of my other friends had showed up," Frank said, "I am certain I would not have reacted in the same way, not have had tears well up and been filled with overwhelming nostalgia. Why was Chezzi's presence so moving?"

Frank felt proud to be able to represent his country. He was so appreciative of his good fortune to become an American citizen that much later he assisted others he met through his work overseas that wanted to relocate to the United States. He had helped people from Hong Kong, Czechoslovakia, Israel and Italy find jobs in America. He had sponsored a few. Most who emigrated from Czechoslovakia continued careers in the textile industry.

"I felt so lucky to be an American," Frank told me after winning the award, "to have my children born in America, to be educated in America, to be free to fly a kite on the beach with my grandchildren in America. I feel for those who don't have the same opportunities and who don't know what they are missing."

The next morning—or maybe it was late that night–-Mikhail Gorbachev stopped Frank in the hotel lobby. He congratulated Frank on winning for the United States. I watched Frank puff up and smile. Then Frank's face softened. Something was off.

"What did Gorbachev just say to you?" I asked with my hand on his shoulder. By now Frank had lived in the States for over 60 years. Nobody could tell German was his first language, Hebrew his second and English his third. Still, he had that accent.

"I'm not sure of the exact words," Frank said. "But I know what he meant."

"What did he mean?" I asked. "What did he say?"

263

"'Tell me,' Gorbachev said. 'Where are you from?'"

"'New York,' I said."

"'No,' Gorbachev said. 'Where are you really from?'"

Newly blended family, 1991. Back Row: Joel, Steven Gottlieb, Marilyn's mom & brother, Marilyn, Frank, Hilda, Michael L. & David. Front Row: Michael M., Melissa & June Gottlieb.

Wedding toast:
Frank & Marilyn,
April 21st, 1991.

Marilyn's men, 1991.
Joel & Michael Molinoff with
Frank, Michael & David Levy.

Marilyn's brother Jerry with
Margit's brother Frank.

Second honeymoon in Aspen, Colorado.
Back row: Joel, Frank. Marilyn, Michael L. & Michael M.
Front row: Carolyn & David.

Frank with Shirley & Paul Turner,
longtime client and friends, 1991.

Three men on left: Crivitz town officials,
with Ada, Inge Rohde & Dr. Fritz Rohde,
Marilyn & Frank, 2012.

Frank returning
to Venice, Italy
to feed the
pigeons, 2012.

Our growing blended family in 2009:
Back Row: Jodi, Michael L., Jennifer, Joel,
David, Carolyn, Frank, Marilyn,
Michael M. & Annabelle.
Front Row: Benjamin, Julia, Charlotte, Theo, Yoni,
Eliana & Margalit.

Frank, Ray C. Anderson, founder of Interface & Sergio with the first fibers made using PCC® technology.

United States

„Recycling Post Consumer Carpets"

2.5 million tons of used carpet, that produces poisonous emissions when incinerated, are dumped in to U.S. landfills annually. This is equal to a hole one mile by one mile by 100 feet deep. If left alone, the carpets never disintegrate. Until now, it was very difficult to separate the petrol-based derivatives to allow recycling of both the nylon and polypropylene materials. Post Consumer Carpet Processing Technologies LLC (PCC) has developed a new, simple, clean and highly economical method that separates the nylon fiber from the carpet backing. Based on PCC's patent-pending technology, Interface, the third largest carpet producer in the world, installed the first line of machinery in September 2007. This enables Interface to recycle 15,000 tons of carpet annually and to reuse the recovered materials for new carpet and other products. The energy saved with a single line of recycling machinery corresponds to the heating demand of more than 250 U.S. households annually and another annual savings of 90 million gallons of water. The oil saved is estimated at 174,000 barrels per year per line of machinery, which at today's prices, is about $19 million.

Applicant: Post Consumer Carpet Processing Technologies (PCC)

Frank & Chezzi in Brussels, 2008.

Frank & Sergio accepting their award from Mrs. Maneka Gandhi, Brussels, 2008.

(Photos © 2008 Michael Molinoff)

267

Frank , Mikhail Gorbachev & Sergio in Brussels, 2008.
(Photo © 2008 Michael Molinoff)

Sergio & his wife, Manuela
in Brussels, 2008.
(Photo © 2008 Michael Molinoff)

Frank & Marilyn.
(Photo © 2013 Michael Molinoff)

Post consumer carpets.

Post consumer carpets 2.

Separated post consumer carpet nylon fiber.

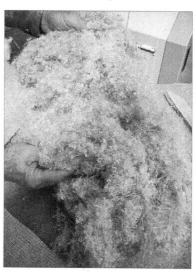

Regenerated nylon fiber.

Sergio & Frank
celebrating their partnership
in Munich, Germany, 2002.

Frank in front of bales of nylon fiber.

Epilogue: With Chezzi and Fritz, 2012

I finished writing this book on May 10, 2012. The next day we flew to Germany to attend two unrelated events that helped me understand Frank's life. The timing was strangely perfect.

The first event was held at Schloss Elmau, one of the most luxurious hotels in Germany, in the Bavarian Alps south of Munich. Swimming in the heated rooftop pool with spring snow tickling my face, breathing in the spectacular environment nestled amidst fields of purple flowers, wide hiking trails, tranquil lakes and imposing mountains, I recognized why the area once was a playground for the Nazis.

We were there to hear Chezzi speak at a seminar featuring successful Jewish writers of German ancestry. Each panelist shared his or her personal story of survival during WWII as well as a synopsis of professional achievements in literature, music, psychoanalysis, journalism and film. Titled, *Judische Portraits*, the seminar was taped by Bayerisches Fernsehen, the Bavarian public broadcasting authority, and was to be aired on German television November 2012.

Every story was different, yet all were the same. The majority of the participants expressed a special feeling for Germany, their motherland. Though most of the ten speakers came from Israel, some claimed to come from a place in their heart or mind or wherever their family was—transplanted people belonging to a group without geographical boundaries, without physical environments or governments.

The seminar was organized by Rachel Salamander, an incredible woman with a long list of credentials. Ms. Salamander was born and raised in a displaced person's camp in Munich. Thirty years before the seminar she started the first Jewish bookstore in Germany. Today there are numerous such stores including one in the visitors' center of the Dachau Concentration Camp Memorial Site.

I asked young Christian people in the audience why they attended. "Guilt about grandparents activities or non activities in WWII" was often the answer. One man told me his parents had helped Jews escape to Sweden or Switzerland. When the war ended, the majority of Germans fell upon hard times. The Jews who had escaped sent packages of food to his family.

The second part of our journey gave us a chance to reunite with Dr. Fritz Rohde and his wife, Inge, from Crivitz, Germany. In honor of the town's 760th anniversary, town officials held a special ceremony in the local church honoring the Jews of Crivitz—people who had been forced to flee or been killed in WWII. Most of the town's Jews were members of Frank's maternal ancestors, the Jacobson family. The event was organized by an ex-Nazi officer who told us he had to arrange this memorial because he felt so guilty about his past. We never found out details.

Frank's sister Ada and her husband Don also attended, as did their second cousin Tova Manor and her

271

husband, Israel. This was the first time Frank and his sister had met Tova.

Prior to the ceremony we walked along the lake where Frank's grandfather had enjoyed ice-skating. We strolled along Parchimerstrasse and snapped photos in front of the Jacobson store. Gertrud Ganz, and her husband Robert, came from Hannover. Their daughter, Judith, came from Cologne and their son and granddaughter came from Hamburg. Gertrud had lived next to the Jacobson store. Her grandparents had owned a bakery across the street where the Jacobsons used to purchase sweets. Hilda had spoken about that bakery where she bought meringue dipped in chocolate for the equivalent of five cents.

After WWII Crivitz was swallowed up by the Russians and became part of East Germany. One of the women had managed to flee to the West just before the borders were closed.

Her friend, Dr. Rohde, had remained in Crivitz. Over dinner in his home, Dr. Rohde explained that the DDS Stasi police had confiscated his house and for years he and his family had experienced their own hard times.

The next day Frank delivered a speech, in German, in the local church. Later he translated it for me.

"As you can see," he said, "we somehow consider Crivitz an important part of the puzzle of our forefathers and our family. Somehow, despite the terrible recent history, we feel for our motherland. On some level, we feel connected and that we belong here."

Before we left, Dr. Rohde removed a photo from his wall in his living room. It was the same photo he had shown us ten years before at lunch in the lakeside restaurant. Dr. Rohde had bought the photo in 1945 from the local butcher. It showed Eduard Jacobson, Frank's great grandfather, looking through the window of the

Jacobson store. Other members of the family are standing in front.

Eduard had eight children. The Nazis killed five. Frank's grandfather, Martin, left before borders were closed. Tova's grandfather, Alfred, had perished defending Germany in WWI, but his three children later escaped the Nazis by fleeing to Palestine. Lulu, the eldest brother, also moved to Palestine.

"I believe your family will treasure this image more than ours will," Fritz said as he gave Frank the photo. Then he drove us to Achim Kröger, a local artist, where we purchased an oil painting of the same scene.

Waiting for the train to Berlin, I watched Frank and Fritz, two friends hugging, tears in the eyes of both men.

I saw that on many levels the past matters.

Parchimerstrasse, the main street in Crivitz, Germany, 1900. The first building on the left was owned by Frank's ancestors from 1740 until WWII. Frank's maternal great grandfather, Eduard Jacobson, can be seen looking out the side window. Frank's grandfather, Martin Jacobson, was born in 1872 in the living quarters above the store.

In1945, Dr. Fritz Rohde, a local vetrinarian in Crivitz, bought the above photo from a woman in town. It hung on his living room wall for 67 years, up until he gave it to Frank in 2012.

Frank with Marilyn, flying his handmade kite in the Hamptons
on Long Island, New York.
(Photo © 2013 Michael Molinoff)

Acknowledgments

This book evolved under the instruction of:
Jules Feiffer, Neal Gabler, Ursula Hegi, Kaylie Jones,
Annette Handley-Chandler, Cindy Kane, Matt Klam, Roger
Rosenblatt, Lou Ann Walker and John Westermann.

Special thanks to:
Lou Ann Walker, author of *A Loss for Words*, professor at
Stony Brook Southampton and editor of *The Southampton
Review*, for her guidance and constant encouragement. I
couldn't have asked for a better mentor or friend.

Ken Roman, former Chairman and CEO of Ogilvy &
Mather Worldwide and author of *The King of Advertising*,
for his advice to treat a final draft as a rough draft and
rewrite it again.

Jean Hazelton, attorney and fellow student at Stony Brook
Southampton, for encouraging me to continue with my
writing in a formal program.

Ana Daniel, history professor, for her support with all
historical references.

Odette Heideman, editor of *Epiphany* literary journal, for
her inspiring review.

Ellen Sax, President of Table Artisty and past President of Boston Wedding Group, for her editorial input.

Dan Rattiner, founder and editor-in-chief of *Dan's Papers* and author of *In the Hamptons,* for publishing my first creative non-fiction columns.

Michael Molinoff, photographer and photo artist, for his photos and keen eye.

Harriet Brownstein, Honorary Board Member of the Anti-Defamation League and a member of the Board of Directors of the Sisterhood of Park East Synagogue, NYC. She also is my sister-in-law, June's, mother. Harriet's wisdom helped me to have patience and to believe Frank and I would have a future together.

Kathleen Lynch of Black Kat Design, for her talent and wonderful disposition.

Bernice Kanner, columnist and author of *Are You Normal* and *The Super Bowl of Advertising,* for being my guiding light when I entered the world of advertising.

Janine Gordon, President and CEO, Janine Gordon Associates, for showing me how to strive for perfection even if it can't be reached.

Robert Reeves and the Stony Brook Southampton family, for helping me to write this book from my husband's memories and search for his roots.

Sheryl Heller and TwinPeaks Geeks for instant aid, with a smile, for every IT emergency.

Lois Regan, expert teacher, for editorial comments.

Special mention to:
Stefano Coppini, Prato, Italy, for inspiring the structure of this book. It has been an honor to discuss literature with him.

Thank you to my tireless first draft readers:
Sarah Azzara, Laurel Bauer, Constance Bennett, Jennifer Brooke, Christopher Cascio, Genevieve Crane, Ana Daniel, Rosemarie Dios, Diana Ghallagher, Penny Knapp, Mitchell Kriegman, Bette Lacina, Monica Leeds, Eileen Obser, Rebecca Packard, Valerie Scopaz, Terry Sullivan, Violet Turner and Jack Werner.

Much appreciation to my second draft readers:
Brian Barrett, Yuval Cohen, Diane and Irwin Friedman, Neil Goldstein, Jean Hazelton, Christiane Heideman, Sheryl Heller, Suzanne Klein, Ofrit Levey, Jennifer Molinoff, Leah Rukeyser, Adrianne Singer and Barbara Schwartz.

Thanks for factual input from:
Laurel Bauer, USA; Dr. Chezzi Cohen, Israel; Professor Ana Daniel, USA: Sergio Dell'Orco, Italy; Gertrud and Judith Ganz, Germany; Benas Levy, South Africa; Tova Manor, Israel; Dr. Ada Olins, USA; Christoph Winterbacher, Austria and our good friend, Dr. Fritz Rohde, in Crivitz, Germany.

Praise for *Life with an Accent*

In *Life With An Accent*, Marilyn Gottlieb explores the complex layers of the past and the present, of the personal and the political.
Ursula Hegi, author, *Children and Fire*

The quality of writing sets a high bar and you feel transported to another world. The structure is remarkable: inventive, metaphorical and succinct. Levy reads like a character out of a novel. It is a truly great read I immediately wanted to share with my mother and my daughter.
Odette Heideman, Editor, *Epiphany,* **a literary journal**

Frank Levy's story, beautifully written by Marilyn Gottlieb, is a true picaresque tale. By turns funny and harrowing, his adventures will leave you marveling at Frank—his persistence, his daring, his wisdom.
Lou Ann Walker, author, *A Loss For Words*

What a brave, innovative narrative. Gottlieb's work captures her husband's restless spirit and his bonhomie while exploring what it takes to survive against the odds. This book is a compelling look at one man's struggle to do good in the world.
Robert Reeves, author, *Doubting Thomas*

Gottlieb's telling of her husband's past is dramatic and inspirational. It is a must read for other immigrants who started over and for all those exploring their own roots.
Linda Goldstein, The Jewish Museum of New York

Part biography, part memoir and part history lesson, Frank Levy's riveting life journey is a compelling read. Immigrants the world over, old and new, will relate to the decision to give up everything and assimilate into a new life is 'not so simple'."
Jeffrey Feinbloom, Feinbloom Bertisch LLP, Immigration Law Specialists

Marilyn Gottlieb gives a human side to the story behind recycling textile waste and used carpets and the importance of saving the environment, not just in the USA, but also in Italy and other countries around the world.
Sergio Dell'Orco, President, Dell'Orco & Villani, manufacturers of textile recycling machinery

This book is a wonderful account of a brilliant businessman and how he survived and thrived. Patience, perseverance and an accumulation of international expertise has allowed Frank Levy to bring global technology to help solve the challenges of carpet recycling in the United States.
Dr. Robert Peoples, Executive Director, Carpet America Recovery Effort, and President, Environmental Impact Group, Inc.

As an immigrant from Egypt I identify with my dear friend, Frank and his quest to reinvent himself. An engineer and inventor of patented technology, he has contributed more than most to American business and sustainability.
Amad Tayebi, Professor Emeritus Plastic Engineering, University of Massachusetts and patent attorney

Book Club Questions

1. Whenever Frank meets someone new he is asked where he is from. Do you know people who speak with a foreign accent? Have you asked them about their experiences as immigrants?

2. Frank's parents chose to leave Germany when they were no longer considered citizens. Under what conditions, if any, would you leave your country?

3. Though they weren't religious, Frank's parents moved to Bat Yam, a more religious community where they sought out other secular Germans. Do you seek friendships with people of a similar background?

4. Though Frank grew up in the Middle East during WWII, he felt he had a peaceful, happy life. How did Frank's parents shield him from political events? Have you ever protected your family from harsh realities? If so, how?

5. Against Frank's wishes, his grandmother brought the family together in America. How did this affect Frank's life? What early experiences were forced upon you as a child? Have you ever imagined living permanently in a foreign country?

6. As a child, Frank showed early signs of strength and independence. How did these strengths help him overcome loss and hardships in his later life? How have you coped with loss?

7. Frank maintained his childhood friendship with Chezzi. How were they able to stay close despite the physical and cultural differences? Have you sustained a close childhood friendship?

8. Frank goes back to his grandparents' village to try to understand his life. Have you ever returned to an old neighborhood or researched the history of your relatives? Did you find the experience satisfying?

9. What is the difference between Frank's childhood experience as an immigrant and your childhood experience? Do you know any children who are immigrants? Are they able to assimilate or do they cling to traditions from their original culture?

10. When Frank decided to find love a second time he searched for a Jewish woman with a German background. Do you think it is important for people in a relationship to have similar backgrounds?

11. Frank has always wanted to help save the land. Were you surprised that he settled on recycling machinery and sustainability as the focus of his career? What childhood dreams did you have and were you able to accomplish them?

12. Hilda was disappointed when Frank married a woman who wasn't German. Why do you think she felt this way? Did you ever experience disappointment in your children's choice of friends or a mate?

13. Frank's grandfather and his dad were his heroes. Frank's dad convinced him to earn a college degree before going back to Israel. Can you think of other ways in which his father and grandfather influenced him? Who are your heroes? Why?

14. At the end of the book Frank becomes friends with the Germans in Crivitz, Germany. Could you become friends with people who might have been involved in violence or discrimination against you and your family? What if those people were caught up in political movements against their will?

15. At the conclusion of the book Frank has created a blended family and developed new technology to help save the environment. Do you think his family values helped him forge his future?

16. America is a land of immigrants. Do you think Frank's experiences are unique or does he parallel the life of many immigrants' lives?

Marilyn Gottlieb

Marilyn Gottlieb started her writing career as a columnist in *Dan's Papers* on Long Island, New York. Since 1993 she has been president of The Crescendo Group, a small full-service public relations firm. Prior to starting her own company, Ms. Gottlieb was senior vice president, director of public relations for Lintas, a $1.8 billion advertising agency. Previously she was with Ogilvy & Mather and the American Association of Advertising Agencies. A past member of the Board of Advertising Women of New York and an inductee into the YWCA's prestigious Academy of Women Achievers, she taught Public Relations at the New School University for 18 years. In 2012 Ms. Gottlieb received an MFA in Writing and Literature from Stony Brook Southampton.

Author photo courtesy of Alessandro Moggi, Prato, Italy.

Thank you

To all the men and women in the Allied Forces
who served during WWII
and enabled me, and my family, to live in freedom

and

To Marilyn, my wife and partner,
for bringing my story to life.

Frank J. Levy

Frank J. Levy.
(Photo © 2008 Michael Molinoff)

Made in the USA
Charleston, SC
09 July 2013